Information-Driven Marketing Decisions

Development of
Strategic Information Systems

A. Coskun Samli

Quorum Books
Westport, Connecticut • London

Library of Congress Cataloging-in-Publication Data

Samli, A. Coskun.
   Information-driven marketing decisions : development of strategic
information systems / A. Coskun Samli.
     p.   cm.
   Includes bibliographical references and index.
   ISBN 0-89930-976-3 (alk. paper)
    1. Marketing—Decision making. 2. Marketing research.
3. Management information systems.   I. Title.
HF5415.135.S26   1996
658.8'02—dc20   95-24086

British Library Cataloguing in Publication Data is available.

Library of Congress Catalog Card Number: 95–24086
ISBN: 0-89930-976-3

First published in 1996

Quorum Books, 88 Post Road West, Westport, CT 06881
An imprint of Greenwood Publishing Group, Inc.

Printed in the United States of America

∞

The paper used in this book complies with the
Permanent Paper Standard issued by the National
Information Standards Organization (Z39.48–1984).

10 9 8 7 6 5 4 3 2 1

This book is dedicated to marketing decision makers
who understand the value of information
and are incessantly in pursuit of it.

Contents

Contents

Exhibits

Preface

Modern business enterprise in the American market is not a kindergarten with computers. It must not be assumed that all the information is there and that thus, if we leave it up to the computer, all necessary decisions will be made automatically and effectively. In recent years, American businesses have performed miracles regarding database development. Indeed, database marketing has become an important concept in American marketing (*Business Week* 1994). Database technology is extremely advanced and very sophisticated (Jackson & Wang 1994). However, this is what is meant by kindergarten with computers. Whereas miracles are performed with data base technology, it is questionable whether the marketing decision maker is being further trained to take advantage of this technology. The people who emphasize the technology have a tendency to forget that marketing decisions cannot, and should not, be made automatically. The availability of data simply creates "a data overload," which has almost no value solely in itself. Data receive their value through their usability by the decision maker. However, technological advances in data generation appear to be diverging away from decision makers and their specific information needs. Instead, because these technologies are advancing rather independently, a tendency is emerging in the direction of developing new technologies that may add to the problem of data overload (Doherty 1993).

Successful marketing in a market system depends on the ability to understand data in order to convert them into useful information and then use this information effectively in the decision-making process. Only properly trained decision makers can use information effectively.

Less well-trained decision makers may not even be able to distinguish between data and information. Soon, everybody in our society and all businesses will have access to unbelievable volumes of data. Although this phenomenon is called the *information superhighway*, I believe that in reality it is a *data superhighway*. This reflects the difference between data and information. Whereas data implies bits of facts, to the firm or the individual decision maker, unless these bits of facts are converted into information on which sound decisions can be made, these data are almost totally useless. This process goes far beyond the data base systems design (Rob & Coronel 1995). It requires a different breed of decision makers who can evaluate the data and understand their information needs. Thus, not those who can get increased volumes of data out of the data superhighway, but rather, those who can convert these data into information, will really benefit from the information revolution that has been going on in the last decade of the twentieth century. Of course, information in itself is of no value unless it is used properly for the decision-making process.

The term "information overload" is, I believe, a total misnomer. Today's U.S. business environment and the decision makers in it are not suffering from an information overload. On the contrary, they are suffering from a data overload and an information underload. No matter how much data are accumulated or accessed, unless converted into information to facilitate the decision-making process, they are of no use. Once the data have been collected, they need to be understood, appreciated, assimilated, processed, formatted, and made available, which transforms them into information.

Thus, the art and science of decision-making is based, first and foremost, on the art and science of information generation, and not solely on data gathering. However, this is only the first step. The decision maker must understand the nature of the information and how it should be used in the decision-making activity, which will determine the fate of the firm in the marketplace. In other words, in order to succeed in today's turbulent markets, a firm must be able to develop a strategic information system and must utilize it fully for successful decision making.

This book dwells on the art and science of information generation and, above all, its utilization for marketing decisions by managers. As Exhibit P–1 illustrates, there is a major set of activities to complete before data can be converted into information. However, the whole process does not stop there. Generating and using information leads to knowledge. This is perhaps the most critical concept in the modern American marketing scene. Not only are the skills to convert data into information lacking, but there is not enough experience and learning based on the decision-making process to lead to knowledge. The current

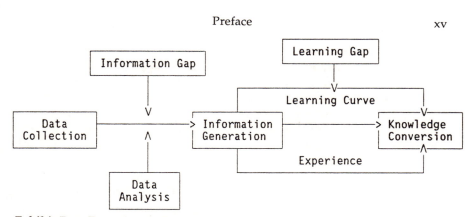

Exhibit P-1 From Data to Knowledge

short-run orientation prevailing in the American corporate entity does not allow, the generation of knowledge based on using information for prolonged periods of time. This situation, combined with the modern American firm's inclination to downsize and turn over the executive talent, is currently causing a lack of knowledge based on information and experience (*Business Week* 1994).

Another factor in this dilemma is related to attempting to use computers to routinize data generation and data use in decision making. This is the danger in using database marketing extensively without the specific input of the marketing decision maker. Decision makers do not stay on the job long enough to develop knowledge, yet it is essential, in today's turbulent American markets, that decision makers understand and use information skillfully and that they gradually develop marketing knowledge. This would enable them to improve their probability of success in the marketplace.

This conversion of information into knowledge is perhaps the most critical factor in marketing decision making. It is based on the premise that good marketing decisions, in the long run, are a function of information and experience as expressed in the form of knowledge, which is, at least partially, based on the learning curve.

Neglecting the process that is displayed in Exhibit P-1 reflects a short-run orientation and an ignorance of the fact that there exists a learning curve between information and knowledge, which illustrates experience with the passage of time. If the experience is not acquired and used properly, in the long run, the life and well-being of the firm will clearly be put in jeopardy.

Thus, as seen in Exhibit P-1, there are two critical gaps between data and knowledge. First, if special input from the marketing decision maker is not interjected, proper information for the firm's needs may fail to develop. Second, if the marketing decision maker does not have enough opportunity to use information and develop knowledge, there will always exist a critical gap between information and knowledge. Here, knowledge includes wisdom. Good information without the wisdom to use it is hardly useful. In time, a firm and its decision makers mature and become wise and knowledgeable. Then, and only then, can information be used in the best possible way. In one way, this book emphasizes the maturing process required for the wisdom and knowledge to make good use of information. Data without information have no value. Similarly, information without the knowledge or wisdom to use it has no value. Thus, both the information gap and the learning gap must be eliminated for a firm to perform exceptionally well in the marketplace.

This book is based on the Exhibit P–1. It emphasizes the process of generating information from data and then converting it into knowledge. Its aim is to provide a framework to eliminate these two dangerous gaps. This whole process would definitely reduce the firm's risks in the face of market adversities and enhance its competitive edge. In essence, the book posits that without information and knowledge, a firm faces a great risk in the marketplace and its probability of survival in the long run is very low. In order to accomplish its goals, the book puts particular emphasis on, first, explaining data generation procedures. Second, information generation procedures are explored. Here, particular emphasis is placed on procedures used to analyze data. Finally, the critical areas of how and why the information must be used are explored. Thus, this book is written for marketing decision makers who wish to use information properly and, in time, develop powerful knowledge in marketing management. The decision maker needs to rely on a strategic information system, which must be functional, in that it generates information and facilitates decision making; accessible, in that the decision maker can retrieve the necessary information; and above all, *decision maker–friendly*, in that it provides the best possible information in the manner needed by the decision maker.

This Preface presents the key elements of the information gap as well as the learning gap that are involved in using data for marketing decisions. Proactive behavior in making information-driven marketing decisions involves, primarily, the elimination of these gaps. This is the subject of this book. The Introduction points out how vital it is to develop an information system in order to survive in the current turbulent American market.

Chapter 1 describes the information evolution in decision making. It focuses on the distinction between data and information. It posits that in order to practice total quality management (TQM), the firm must generate information from the market responses, which requires a carefully balanced information system.

Chapter 2 presents a discussion of the current status of marketing research, including a trend whereby the data gathering and processing techniques are becoming extremely sophisticated, but not necessarily *decision maker–friendly*.

Chapter 3 provides a discussion of various techniques used in collecting data and, furthermore, discusses specific ways of generating information from data.

Chapter 4 explores different dimensions of internal data and some of their parameters. How these data are used properly for marketing decisions is one of the most important points in marketing decision making.

Chapter 5 discusses one of the best, but also the most understated, data-gathering methods: observation. The marketing decision maker must become very familiar with this effective and low-cost technique.

Chapter 6 explores different dimensions of the most common data gathering technique in marketing: surveys. The discussion shows that different survey techniques have different strengths and weaknesses.

Chapter 7 dwells on an expensive and complicated data gathering technique: experimentation. It puts forth some special details relating to test marketing of which the marketing decision maker must be aware.

Chapter 8 analyzes some of the important aspects of attitude research with which marketing decision makers must be familiar. In marketing, understanding attitudes can lead to important predictions.

Chapter 9 uncovers the key aspects of motivation research and explains how data are collected through various techniques related to this research area. Understanding motives behind the behavior patterns is very critical for the marketing decision maker.

Chapter 10 explores a commonly ignored area, the management of marketing research. If marketing research activity is not managed well, it cannot generate good information for decision making.

Chapter 11 analyzes just how information is developed from data. Here, various statistical techniques used in data analyses are contrasted from the decision maker's point of view.

Chapter 12 posits that using the information generated from the data is the most critical area in the discussion of marketing information systems. It identifies the critical marketing decision areas and explains how information is used in each.

Chapter 13 deals with the control mechanism and reiterates the point that the information system must work well. Feedback leading to corrective action through the control mechanism is extremely critical in successful marketing.

Finally, the "Postscript" puts forth a research agenda to improve the information-driven marketing decision process and reinforces the importance of having a dynamic information system that facilitates marketing decision making.

REFERENCES

"Data Base Marketing." 1994. *Business Week*, September 5, 56–62.
Doherty, Stephen A. 1993. "Emerging Technologies." *Internal Auditor*, December, 18–25.
Jackson, Rob, and Paul Wang. 1994. *Strategic Database Marketing*. Lincolnwood, IL: NTC Business Books.
Rob, Peter, and Carlos Coronel. 1995. *Data Base Systems*. Danvers, MA: Boyd and Fraser.

Acknowledgments

Many people contributed directly and indirectly to the development of this book. Early on, my thinking was formed with the aid of the meticulous tutelage of Professor Stanley Hollander of Michigan State. While at that university, I was fortunate to be a research assistant at the Bureau of Business Research, where I was involved in various research projects. Special gratitude must be given to Professor David Luck, who gave me my first job, as a Research Assistant at Michigan State University.

I have taught marketing research in more than half a dozen universities for more than twenty-five years. All throughout this period, I felt the deficiency in the literature regarding how research findings must be used by decision makers. After all, if the decision makers fail to use the information generated by research, what is its value?

In many meetings and workshops that I conducted with practitioners, decision makers and entrepreneurs, I realized that there is a natural (or unnatural) fear of marketing research. Without good decisions, businesses cannot survive in the marketplace.

My friend, colleague, and coauthor of many years, Professor Joe Sirgy, has always been available to argue or interact. Many times, and very patiently, he has coped with some of my outrageous ideas and brought me back to earth.

My other colleagues at the University of North Florida, knowingly or otherwise, have been pulled into many discussions pertaining to various points in this book. In particular, Professor Steve Paulson of the University of North Florida deserves much credit. He read each chapter and made valuable comments, which were subsequently incorporated into the book.

My friend and coauthor, James Myers, originally was instrumental in developing some of the important areas in Chapter 10. Our work has attracted much attention.

Professors Bruce Kavan and Cheryl Frohlich, in addition to coauthoring a section in Chapter 1, have been very helpful in discussing many issues of this book. Indeed, they are always helpful. My Dean, Earle Traynham, has been particularly helpful by providing me with the necessary support to write this book. My department head, Dr. Robert Pickhardt, also has always been available for encouragement and support.

This book could not have been written without the research help received from my graduate assistant, N. Mehmet Ongan, who has refined his research skills in such a way that I had outstanding support for all the chapters in this book. He also painstakingly read my chapters and developed my index.

Our department secretaries, Gwen Bennett and Betty Geitz, were always there to help. However, once again, nobody's contribution has been as great as that of my secretary, Leanna Payne, who not only typed from my hardly legible handwritten notes, but also carefully read every word in every chapter. As usual, I always sought her seal of approval, which I value very highly.

Hundreds of my graduate students listened, reacted, argued, and sometimes disagreed with me about my points that are made in this book. They were patient enough to listen to my, at times, rather out-of-the-ordinary ideas. I owe them much. Beverly Chapman, as in the previous books, gave me a helping hand in editing this volume as well. Finally, Bea Goldsmith read, argued, and advised me to come back to reality in many parts of this book. Her contributions are quite visible in this volume, as they were in my previous volumes.

To these and many other people who, over the years, discussed, interacted, or researched these issues with me, I extend my deep gratitude. I hope that this book, by making a modest but noticeable contribution, will be a payoff for their trouble. Many, many years of hard work, consulting, and research activity went into its preparation. My most important wish regarding this book is that marketing decision makers have access to it and benefit by reading it and using some of its ideas.

Introduction

Some years ago, Peter Drucker (1989), in describing the American economy, talked about the New Information Society. A few years earlier, Naisbitt (1982) had already referred to the ongoing transition in American society as a major switch from an industrial to an information society. In order to understand this book, it is necessary to understand the new information society. This chapter deals with the concept. Throughout this chapter and this book, a critical distinction between data and information is emphasized. Information is data that is organized, analyzed, and formatted according to the needs of the business in question. Without this information, business decisions are bound to be haphazard and risky.

THE NEW INFORMATION SOCIETY

Ever since the development of computers, society has not been the same. Knowing that all decisions are based on a certain type or form of information, decision makers have improved their chances of making better decisions. Better decisions will: (1) improve the firm's competitive advantage, (2) enable it to cope with the prevailing turbulence in the American markets, and (3) empower it to survive in chaos.

Information and Competitive Advantage:

Since information is bits of data pertaining to the circumstances under which decisions need to be made, it is critical that a firm use these data accurately and effectively so that its ability to compete in the marketplace is enhanced. The firm that does not understand what its opportunities are, the threats it is facing, its strengths and weaknesses and, accordingly, what its priorities should be (Samli 1993) cannot possibly make good decisions on how to enhance a competitive advantage. These activities require, not just data, but data that are analyzed, processed, and formatted to facilitate the decision-making process. This transforms it from indiscriminate bits of data to information that will adequately facilitate the decisions that need to be made.

Information and Turbulence

The American economy is depicted as one that is experiencing constant turbulence (Samli 1993). As Drucker (1989, 2) states: "Turbulence, by definition, is irregular, non-linear, erratic. But its underlying causes can be analyzed, predicted, managed." Herein lies the importance of information. In order to analyze, predict, and manage, the firm must first gather data and then convert them into information suitable for effective decision making. However, studies indicate that poor planning and use of information lead to inferior performance in turbulent markets (Glaser & Weiss 1993). Exhibit I–1 identifies some of the key sources of the prevailing turbulence in the American market. It also illustrates the type of information needed to enable a firm to cope with this turbulence. Finally, the exhibit illustrates the source of such information.

There are at least nine factors causing turbulence: (1) business cycles, (2) declining competition, (3) the move toward an information society, (4) foreign competition, (5) a changing power situation, (6) changing lifestyles, (7) political impact, (8) downsizing, and (9) bottom-lining.

American business cycles have been in existence for a long time. However, it has been stated that in recent years they have become deeper and last longer. Furthermore, it is claimed that recovery on the part of the American economy is becoming increasingly weaker. From the firm's perspective, it is necessary to determine how business cycles influence the firm's target markets. Based on this information, the firm can modify its marketing strategy. Consumer studies before, during, and after the recession, as they relate to the firm's products, are a major source of, first, data and, then, information. Secondary data of consumer consumption patterns also provide a good source of information for a firm. Data on business cycle development data can be used to develop information about the firm's performance during recessions.

Declining competition is a critical factor in the American economy and is causing powerful changes in the marketplace. Through mergers and acquisitions, large firms in America are gaining control over the markets and the nature of competition is changing. The challenge of

	Type of Information	Source of Information
Business Cycles	The relationship of early economic indicators to the firm's performance.	Department of Commerce data are analyzed in view of the firm's performance. Consumer studies to determine the impact of recessions.
Declining Competition	All the merger and acquisition activity and other related activity and their impact on the firm's market position.	News, Wall Street, Federal Trade Commission, Securities Exchange Commission, and others.
Access to Information	Competitors' capability in acquiring and utilizing information.	Associates in the field; networks, computer system suppliers, information generators.
Foreign Competition	The market power of foreign products or services. Possible changes in this picture.	International trade data, industry data worldwide, networking.
Changing Power Structure	Increasing or decreasing oligopolistic market conditions. Concentration of economic power.	Number of competitors and their relative market share. Mergers and acquisitions and their newly acquired power.
Changing Life Styles	Most recent consumer or customer trends. Their implication for the firm. How do these modify the firm's market opportunities?	Customer analysis. Original market and consumer studies, secondary consumption data.
Political Impact	The present state and federal governments' attitude toward competition. How do these attitudes impact the firm's market opportunities?	Economic plans of states and federal government. Time series analyses (trends); historical inferences.
Downsizing	How do layoffs affect the firm's and its competitors' market competitiveness? Human resource development strategy of the firm and its competitiveness.	Consumer evaluation analysis of the firm and its competitors. Comparative market performance analysis.
Bottom-lining	How restrictive is it to emphasize short-run returns of the firm, rather than overall long-term performance?	Impact analysis of financial restrictions on the firm's market performance. Competitors' financial strategies.

Exhibit I–1 Causes of Turbulence and the Firm's Information Needs

competing with large firms is quite different from competing with small firms. Determining the changing and declining competition will provide direction for the firm's marketing plan and indicate how it must be revised. Knowing, for instance, that there are fewer competitors and that they are larger than before may impel the firm to think about more niching and being more effective in its niching efforts. In other words, when there are only a few very large firms (an oligopoly), it may be difficult for an existing small firm to survive. If such a firm can find a narrowly defined segment of the market (a niche) for itself, it improves its chances for survival.

Part of the information that is needed would be obtained from all the merger and acquisition data. The changes that are necessary in the firm's marketing plan will have to be based on information generated internally. Thus, internal information connected to external data provides new dimensions for the firm's marketing activity. Obviously, some data are generated externally, and some, internally. All are transformed into types of information that can be used most effectively.

Access to information becomes increasingly critical as society shifts from an industrial to an information society. Access to information is partially related to the firm's orientation toward an appreciation of information. If it can generate a large amount of data, convert them into information, and use this information effectively, the firm is most likely to improve its competitive advantage. Much of the information generation activity is related to the firm's ability to create proper access to data and to generate information. The information, of course, is generated from a large variety of internal and external sources.

Foreign competition is, and has been, on the rise and is creating a substantial amount of turbulence in American markets. It is necessary for a firm to monitor its market position vis-à-vis the foreign competition. Determining the changes in these relationships and predicting their impact on the firm's profit picture is critical. Thus, it is important to follow closely the trends in international trade and other international industry data worldwide.

As competition declines, the power structure changes. Changes in the power structure cause powerful repercussions. An increase or decrease in the oligopolistic nature of the industry is likely to impact that industry's power structure. If a firm is not cognizant of such changes, it may find itself competing with forces that it cannot match or cope with. The firm must follow closely the numbers and the power of its competitors. As new oligopolies emerge, the outcomes of mergers and acquisitions need to be monitored so that the expected impact of the newly acquired power can also be kept in check.

Changing lifestyles of consumers are sending shock waves throughout some of the traditional consumer product industries. It is critical for firms to diagnose these trends early and determine their implication. There are always new market opportunities, along with disappearing markets. The firm must continuously analyze consumer purchasing behavior and consumption patterns. It also must generate internal data revealing the firm's market position in a changing industry.

Politics, and particularly the programs and orientation of the federal and state governments, plays a critical role in the constantly changing and turbulent American economy. The politics of competition, the position that governments take toward enhancing or reducing competition, and their stimulation or stifling of growth in certain industries will create new opportunities and perhaps eliminate others. A firm must consequently monitor the plans of state and federal government in an effort to determine their impact.

Downsizing has been, perhaps, one of the most critical sources of turbulence in the American economy during the late 1980s and early 1990s. As firms downsize, their competitive edge and capabilities change. How do these changes influence the firm's market performance? As the competition changes, what happens to the particular company? Consumer evaluation of the firm's competitiveness, its services, and the quality it delivers are all critical considerations and need to be assessed regularly.

Finally, during the past decade or so, American firms have become extremely cost-conscious. Concern about efficiency is quite acceptable; however, strict cost-consciousness has created critical problems in a firm's ability to deliver quality, to maintain competitive advantage, and to keep its market position. Conducting internal research determining the firm's short-run versus long-run performance and contrasting these with the firm's changing market opportunities is very critical. The firm may undertake an impact analysis of financial restrictions on its performance. It may also contrast these findings with those of its competitors.

The proper use of information can enable a firm to weather adversities in the economic environment. Once again, the generation and utilization of information are critical considerations.

Information and Chaos

The third contribution of the proper use of information is the empowerment of the firm to survive chaos. In describing turbulence, Drucker (1989) stated that the underlying causes can be analyzed, predicted, and managed. If this is not done, there will be chaos. Flower (1993) stated that the word *chaos* describes situations in an organization in which people are confused and feeling overwhelmed with information of which they cannot make sense. In many cases, the American economy is flirting with chaos. It has not been emphasizing infrastructure nor is it developing human resources. It does not have a strategic plan for its industry, and it is allowing the rich to become richer and the poor very poor (Samli 1993). Perhaps information will alert a company to imminent chaos and, if properly used, will avert a firm's collapse. Furthermore, some aspects of chaos may be converted into new opportunities. Information can facilitate a firm's assessment of these new opportunities and its being made more proactive in order to take advantage of them. Bringing order out of chaos is necessary for a firm's survival. Technology first created the opportunity for the mass movement of data and now is developing possible solutions to chaotic conditions. One of these developments is the completely integrated business environment (CIBE). This process tries to integrate all of the various types of information that flow through a business (*Management Accounting*, 1990).

Thus far it has been emphasized that information is needed simply to cope with the adversities of the marketplace. As information becomes more critical, firms are employing increasing numbers of information workers. These are the specialists who not only generate data for the firm but also convert this data into usable information.

INFORMATION WORKERS VERSUS
INFORMATION USERS

Drucker (1989) used the term *information workers* to identify people working in research or management information systems (MIS) and who generate information for the firm. Although these people are very important for a firm's well-being since they generate information for it, they should not be confused with the individuals in the firm who make decisions. In fact, it must be recognized that information is not an end in itself; on the contrary, it is a means to an end. Its purpose is to facilitate the decision-making process.

Although there are many important information (or knowledge) workers, their number is relatively small when compared to the number of information users. All decision makers are information users. Therefore, they need to understand the differences among the concepts of data, information, and knowledge. They are not particularly concerned about the ways in which the information was developed but rather with how this information should be used most effectively. All decisions must be information-based. An awareness of this fact is the first prerequisite of effective decision making.

Exhibit I–2 illustrates how information enters into all stages of the decision-making process. The five-step decision process displayed in the exhibit is rather standard. However, it is critical to note that in each of the five steps, there are information inputs, without which it may be almost impossible to continue. Finally, monitoring the outcome produces information in itself and reinforces the next step of the decision process.

It must be further reiterated that every decision goes through this five-step procedure and that therefore, all decisions require information inputs. Since a firm's functions are based on constant decision-making activity, it becomes obvious that information is a totally inseparable component of survival and success. Decisions that are not based on information have the tendency to be arbitrary and, hence, risky.

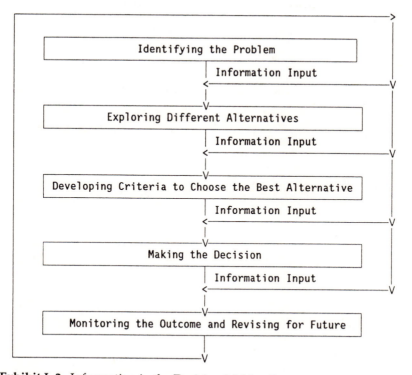

Exhibit I-2 Information in the Decision-Making Process

Perhaps one of the most important considerations in business decision making is that decisions are made to minimize the risk and maximize the probability of capitalizing on market opportunities. The more
information-based the decisions, the more effective they are. Thus, the
use of information can be equated with risk management. The better
the decision, the less the risk and, hence, proper information and its
effective use are imperative for business success.

SUMMARY

This introduction puts the use of information in the proper perspective. Through information, businesses can enhance their competitive
advantage. They can cope with market turbulence and survive chaos.
Whereas there are relatively few (but important) information workers
to generate information for the decision-making process, there are
many decision makers, who are information users. The use of informa-

tion in the decision-making process not only enhances the effectiveness of decisions but also helps minimize risks for the firm.

REFERENCES

"Bringing Order Out of Chaos." 1990. *Management Accounting—London*, September, 16–17.

Drucker, Peter. 1989. *The New Realities*. New York: Harper and Row.

Flower, Joe. 1993. "The Power of Chaos." *Healthcare Forum*, September/October, 48–55.

Glaser, Rashi, and Allen M. Weiss. 1993. "Marketing in Turbulent Environments: Decision Processes and the Time-Sensitivity of Information." *Journal of Marketing Research* (November) 509–21.

Naisbitt, John. 1982. *Megatrends*. New York: Warner Books.

Samli, A. Coskun. 1993. *Counterturbulence Marketing*. Westport, CT: Quorum Books.

The Information Evolution in Decision Making

INTRODUCTION

Marketing decision makers have always understood that they need to remain close to their markets. Today, this closeness can be achieved by information technology (IT). By building powerful customer information systems, companies not only can understand individual consumers better, they can also identify new markets and develop new and better products (Bessen 1993).

Today, with the sophisticated new systems of information technology, companies can take advantage of the following factors:

1. Databases are far larger today than they were even in the fairly recent past. They may include information on tens of millions of households.
2. The depth of information generated from databases on individuals and households can be much greater.
3. This information can be used as part of a highly automated business function.

Points (2) and (3) are particularly important. While there are more data, there is also a greater tendency to use automated data analysis and to make decisions based on highly automated information systems. I maintain in this book that unless data are carefully processed and converted into information and, subsequently, into knowledge, decisions cannot be made effectively. This chapter introduces the current evolution of information, which is directly associated with IT. Information users must understand this evolution and its ramifications.

THERE IS NEVER ENOUGH MARKETING INFORMATION

Despite recent developments in IT, there typically exists insufficient marketing information. The reason confusion prevails is that there is no distinction made between marketing data and marketing information. Because of the advances in IT, the problem is one, not of *information overload*, but of *data overload*. Marketing information is generally scarce because marketing decision makers may not be in a position to ask for information that is critical for their decisions. Additionally, information workers in the company, as well as its computer specialists, may opt to put out large databases without converting the data into marketing information. Considering the dynamic nature of American markets, marketing information will typically be less than adequate.

FROM *EDP* TO *SIS* AND BEYOND

Because American markets are extremely dynamic and American firms need to cope with this dynamism, there has been a continuing search for information and an ongoing evolution in information systems.

Marketing information evolution started with the emergence of management information systems (MIS) as a replacement for electronic data processing (EDP) systems. Alter (1980, xi) stated: "Although the computer industry has enjoyed remarkable success in transforming the way business transactions and data are processed, MIS and management science professionals have been disappointed by the relatively limited use of these systems for managerial decision making."

This situation, at least partially, is responsible for the emergence of decision support systems (DSS) in the early 1970s. DSS are designed specifically to facilitate the decision process. As Alter (1980) stated, they provide flexibility and insight into changing managerial needs. However, businesses need to make decisions in many areas, all of which are not equally important. During the late 1970s and early 1980s, there was a dramatic movement toward placing particular emphasis on strategic planning (Samli 1985; see also Montgomery & Weinberg 1979; Cravens 1982). The changing emphasis on information needs brought about the development of strategic information systems (SIS).

	EDP	MIS	DSS	SIS
Purpose	Improve efficiency in gathering and organizing and analyzing data for business transactions.	Developing information systems specifically for management's use.	Applying information systems to the decision problems of management.	Providing critical information particularly geared to developing and implementing strategies.
Database	Broad database for all aspects of business transactions.	Broad database for all types of management problem areas.	Specific database for all management decisions.	Specific database processed for and related strategy development and implementation.
Orientation	Improving efficiency of the firm units' efforts to gather data for business transactions.	Developing an information system which would help management in all aspects.	Facilitates the firm's decision making process with a supportive information system.	Making available the information system that is necessary for strategic planning.
Features	Access to all kinds of information. Ability to process the data. Ability to retrieve information.	Access to external and environmental data. Access to internal data needed for management. Ability to retrieve. Ability to update and purge.	Ability to manipulate and process data and generate new data. Access to internal data. Ability to retrieve. Ability to update and purge.	Ability to manipulate and generate futuristic data. Ability to access effectiveness of past activities readily to provide control data.

Source: Samli (1985)

Exhibit 1–1 Evolution in Information Systems

Exhibit 1–1 illustrates a comparative analysis of these four stages in the information evolution: EDP, MIS, DSS, and SIS. As can be seen, each stage is different and serves a different purpose.

While EDP improves efficiency by gathering, organizing, and analyzing data for business transactions, MIS develops information systems specifically for the management's use. DSS, on the other hand, applies information systems to specific decision areas that management is facing. Finally, SIS provides critical information that is particularly geared to developing and implementing strategies.

EDP capitalizes on a broad database for all aspects of the business and its transactions. MIS also has a broad database, which is utilized for all types of management problem areas. DSS provides (or, better yet, requires) databases for all management decisions. SIS uses more specific databases for strategy development and implementation.

In terms of orientation, EDP can improve the efficiency of a firm's efforts. It gathers data for all the firm's transactions and may be able to improve their effectiveness in some cases. MIS is oriented to developing a general information system that would primarily help the management of the firm. DSS facilitates the firm's decision-making process by developing an information system that will support all kinds of decisions. Finally, SIS makes available the particular information system necessary for strategic planning exclusively.

These four points in the evolutionary process have different features. EDP has access to all kinds of information and has the ability to process the data into information. It can retrieve the data, the information, or both. MIS has access to external and environmental data. It also has access to internal data that are needed for management. It develops databases for management, and it retrieves, updates, and purges them. Finally, SIS has the ability to manipulate and generate futuristic data and to assess the effectiveness of the past activities and establish controls.

This evolution continues. In recent years, expert systems (ES) emerged as another focal point. However, unlike the four distinct points discussed in the evolutionary process (i.e., EDP, MIS, DSS, and SIS), ES applies to all of them.

EXPERT SYSTEMS

Expert systems are computer systems that use the experience of one or more experts in some problem domain and apply their problem-solving capabilities to make useful inferences for the system user (Mentzer & Gandhi 1992). The knowledge base essentially is built on certain rules and facts that come from expertise. Expert systems are built interactively. There has been a tendency in information technology to develop routinized shells that can be used by the marketing practitioner. In order to illustrate the utilization of ES, a model can be constructed. Exhibit 1–2 is such a model, and although it was constructed to depict the structure of market response to the software industry, it can also be utilized for many other businesses. In a similar model (Arinze 1990),

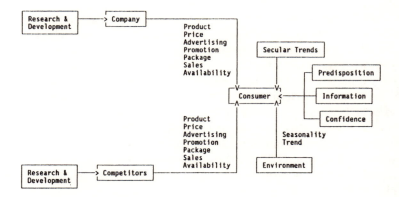

Source: Adapted and revised from: Arinze 1990.

Exhibit 1–2 Structure of a Market Model *Source:* Adapted and revised from Arinze (1990).

	Data and Information Needs	Expected Outcome
Company	The impact and effectiveness of the company's marketing mix components	Better market position, stronger competitive advantage
Competitors	The impact and effectiveness of their marketing mix components	To improve the firm's own competitive advantage
Consumers	Understanding the key critical factors in the consumer behavior pattern	Providing better satisfaction for customers, creating greater loyalty toward the company and its products
Secular Trends	Determining key trends in the market and how they influence the firm	Diversification, product and service adjustment, greater customer satisfaction, risk reduction
Seasonality Trends	Determining the seasonal characteristics of the firm's business	Developing counter seasonal trends, more diversification
Environment	Environmental implications of the firm's products and/or services	Changing product design, product content services, diversification

Exhibit 1–3 Data and Subsequent Information Needs for the Market Response Model

computerized databases designed to support the marketing function at an expert system development company were generated.

The model in Exhibit 1–2 is based on market response and competitive conditions and will interactively provide the best marketing mix alternatives. The critical point, of course, is the system's level of expertise. Consequently, those who develop the expert system need to understand the response pattern in the marketplace. It must be noted that data based on this model can be substantially varied and may be functional or dysfunctional. For instance, the company may put all its emphasis on understanding the relative roles of the key variables listed in the exhibit as components of the marketing mix. This will emphasize primarily internal information, at the expense of external information. This situation may be somewhat modified and rectified if the firm is also keeping track of the market mix of its competition, which will require additional external information.

Exhibit 1–3 illustrates other areas of emphasis that require external data. For instance, the consumer component of the model, at least, requires three bits of data: (1) consumer predisposition, (2) consumer information, and (3) consumer confidence.

While consumer predisposition is related to corporate image, store image, or product image, consumer information may include product protection, product use, resource preservation, environmental friendliness, price information, and many other aspects. Finally, consumer confidence here is meant to be the overall outlook of consumers toward the economy, their own future, and their attitude regarding the economic conditions.

Similarly, certain secular trends, such as the utilization of personal computers (PCs) in the home, health-consciousness, and many other "megatrends" (Naisbitt 1982) need to be taken into consideration. Some of these may have a direct and dramatic impact on the firm, while others may have only milder and indirect impact. However, they all must be sorted out and the information must be fed into the system. These additional bits of information make the expert system increasingly dependent on external information. This is a costly proposition, but such additional information can enable decision makers to optimize their decisions and enhance their competitive advantage.

It is very early to judge the importance and the role of expert systems. It appears at this point that they are an improvement in information technology and could enhance the effectiveness of all EDP, MIS, DSS, and SIS. If the system exceeds the capabilities of SIS and is used exclusively for strategic decision making, then it may take its rightful place in the evolution of information systems. What marketing research users need to understand is that information workers (or researchers) will provide data banks. However, it is up to the research user to make decisions as to information needs, quality of the information, and how it can be used. This book is designed to enhance the research user's skills in using the data and coping with the uncertainties of the marketplace by using the firm's information systems for better marketing decisions.

BALANCED INFORMATION SYSTEMS[1]

As can be seen, information systems (IS) are evolving. While theoretically and conceptually they are maturing and adding to their capabilities, they are also developing the basis for gaps. A gap in this case is the difference between what the IS can provide and what the firm is using. Kavan, Frohlich, and Samli (1994) illustrated this with an example from the banking industry. They maintained that due to excessive

1. This section up to TQM is written jointly by A. Coskun Samli, Bruce Kavan, and Cheryl Frohlich.

emphasis on a bottom-line orientation, banks have focused primarily on attaining the internal efficiency associated with reducing operational expense (*ABA Banking Journal* 1991). Improved efficiency reduces the cost of operations and has an immediate effect on profitability. The banking industry's confusion between efficiency and effectiveness has resulted in a gap created by the utilization of internal information concerning efficiency as a proxy for measuring effectiveness. This substitution has often resulted in a reduction of service quality compared to what the customers expect. An increased number of dissatisfied customers ultimately translates into reduced long-term opportunities for revenue. Increasing internal efficiency without considering the needs of a bank's customers (external opportunities) results in the bank becoming less effective in providing customer satisfaction (Gronroos 1990; Samli & Frohlich 1992). Optimizing market performance, not simply in banking but in any business, is basically related to the fit between the organization's marketing strategy and its information system. In order for such a fit to be optimized, the information system has to be properly balanced. This particular balance is likely to be industry-specific. Furthermore, the balance will vary based on the economic conditions and the comparative structure within an industry. That is, one industry may require a greater amount of internal information relative to external information than another firm for each to find its proper balance. Within these constraints, there may be other conditions dictating the nature of the firm's information system. Researchers and research users must get together and decide just what information is required to make optimal decisions for the firm.

DEVELOPING A BALANCED INFORMATION SYSTEM

An organization's excessive emphasis on efficiency, coupled with inadequate market research and deficient customer orientation (Zeithaml, Berry, & Parasuraman 1988), are quite likely to contribute to a negative cycle in the company's profit picture or an oscillation in profits. This negative picture is caused by the temporary illusional relief in terms of declining costs by reducing short-term operational expenses, but at the expense of long-term effectiveness or profitability. In systems theory terms: "the feedback is less than the output. Unstable oscillation is caused by a feedback signal that induces corrective action greater than the error and thus amplifies the original disturbance" (Schaderbek 1985, 108). Therefore, the problem is systemic in nature and will require a considerable reorientation of management's thinking to reverse. In order to achieve this reversal it is necessary to identify the

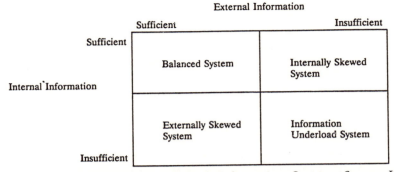

Exhibit 1–4 Developing a Balanced Information System. *Source:* Kavan, Frohlich, and Samli, *"Developing a Balanced Information System," in Journal of Services Marketing 8(1), 1994. By permission.*

alternatives. Exhibit 1–4 illustrates that there are four generic information systems. Three of these four systems are likely to contribute to oscillating profits, and at least two are likely to represent a situation where the feedback is less than the output. As seen in Exhibit 1–4, there are four alternative systems: (1) internally skewed. (2) externally skewed, (3) information underload, and (4) balanced. These are all generic information system alternatives.

An internally skewed system emphasizes operating efficiency (sufficient internal information) to the detriment of effectiveness (which requires a balance between internal and external information). This generic information system is quite likely to contribute to an oscillating profit picture and create a situation in which the feedback is less than the output. The banking sector, for instance, could be placed in the upper right quadrant (internally skewed system). The banking information system has failed to adequately respond to a changing external environment, as evidenced by the escalation in the number of bank failures and the industry's declining rate of return on investment in the late 1980s and early 1990s. With increased accounting sophistication supported by improving information technology, not only the banking industry, but many other American industries as well may be classified in this category. This is due to the temptation to use more internal data and manipulate them into information rather easily.

An externally skewed system is one that has sufficient external information but lacks sufficient internal information for decision purposes. This generic information system alternative is also quite likely to contribute to profit oscillations and inadequate feedback. Consider as an example a service organization that has done an outstanding analysis of potential market opportunity but fails to reconcile the introduction or the delivery of the types of products that this market requires with the organization's current capabilities. For example, the entry of American Telephone and Telegraph (AT&T) into the credit card business provided a desirable product but at an initial expense that was unacceptable to the company. The company, therefore, had to draw back on its marketing campaign and limited national advertising (*Florida Times Union* 1993, *Wall Street Journal* 1992).

An information-underloaded system includes the industry or company that has strictly insufficient data from either internal and external sources. These companies or industries are placed in the lower right quadrant. This is another information system that causes profit oscillations. However, both its output and its feedback are inadequate. Hence, the system is neither efficient nor effective. This concept may be illustrated by the response of thrifts to the Monetary Control Act of 1980 and the Garn–St. Germain Act of 1982. These legislative attempts to allow thrifts to diversify their asset base were met by the almost immediate entry by the thrifts into commercial real estate lending, even though most of these service organizations had neither the internal skills to lend in the commercial area nor the external knowledge of the commercial real estate market. Thus, poor underwriting resulted in the overbuilding of commercial property due to an underutilization of both internal and external information.

As seen in Exhibit 1–4, the only option that provides optimal outcome is the upper left quadrant (balanced system). This particular generic option implies the proper balance between the internal and external information content in the service organization's information system. The critical point in this concept is balance. However, balance should not be construed as a one-to-one ratio between external and internal information. For example, five units of external information and five units of internal information may not create a perfect balance. In some circumstances, such as the service organization, external information may be needed more readily than internal information. Thus, the balance between the two types of information may be two units of external information for every one unit of internal information. On the other hand, if the company is a manufacturing firm (such as a steel mill) as opposed to a service organization (such as a bank), the need for internal information will likely be substantially greater in order for the company to be effective. Consequently, the balancing of the information system may mean a disproportionate use of internal or external information, depending on the industry.

Another factor that influences the information system's balance is related to general economic conditions. In economic down- and upturns, the firm's need for external information changes. Many firms are not quite cognizant of their changing needs for information. Unless there is

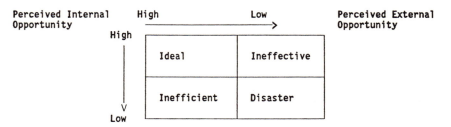

Exhibit 1-5 The Firm's Assessment of Opportunities

a certain amount of understanding and sensitivity, it is not possible for them to develop or maintain a balanced information system.

Finally, a third cause of inability to develop a balanced information system is the firm's internal bias. Exhibit 1–5 illustrates this situation. If a firm, for instance, goes for a low external opportunity option because it does not have the expertise to obtain good external data, all its products or services will be keyed to the wrong market segments; thus, its marketing activity will be ineffective. Similarly, if the firm's assessment of its own internal opportunities is not realistic, then it will be inefficient. It may be producing wrong products, cutting the wrong costs, or laying off the wrong people. In all these cases, the firm may perform inefficiently.

The "disaster" area in Exhibit 1–5 illustrates a firm's inability to assess both internal and external opportunities. A totally inadequate information system, thus, is conceived to be disastrous. Of course, the opposite of this situation is the upper left quadrant in Exhibit 1–5, which is identified as the ideal situation. Here, a well-balanced and functional information system provides the firm with the proper decision parameters and enables it to function optimally. Therefore, it is clear that a balanced information system is necessary in order to optimize performance.

THE RECENT UPSURGE OF MIS

Despite the fact that there are many different forms of IS, such as EDP, MIS, DSS, SIS, and perhaps ES, during the past decade all the work that has taken place in the information systems area has been classified under the umbrella of MIS. Regardless of what the whole effort may be termed, with the development of information technology in both the hardware and software areas, there has been a tendency to analyze data more carefully and, perhaps, more skillfully. Again, if we review the concept of a balanced information system, it becomes clear that the advanced sophistication to generate and manipulate data could be either a tremendous support or a critical danger. The recent upsurge in information technology an MIS does not make this point clearly. Data overload does not help the firm. In fact, as seen in Exhibits 1–4 and 1–5, it can be rather dangerous. Thus, a self-destructive MIS is something to watch for and avoid.

THE SELF-DESTRUCTIVE INFORMATION SYSTEM

If the information system is not properly open to the outside world and is only used in generating and manipulating data, the imbalance may be destructive. Because of the existing accounting data and the fascination with various software to manipulate them, in recent years there have been attempts to develop information systems that are primarily or exclusively internal data–oriented. Much of the time, the finance and accounting staffs who are manipulating these data are either not sufficiently informed about marketing data or not quite capable of obtaining the necessary data. Thus, the systems that are emerging from these efforts are dangerous and self-destructive. If not put into a real-world context, in time, internal data will become irrelevant and totally misleading.

THE TQM CRAZE

During the 1980s, total quality management (TQM) swept U.S. corporate boardrooms (*Business Week*, August 8, 1994). Although I think of TQM as nothing more than proactive marketing, it is important to realize that over and beyond dealing with market turbulence, it provides outstanding opportunities for the firm.

Exhibit 1–6 is, in a sense, a supplement to Exhibit 1–3. It provides the general characteristics of TQM and identifies several information needs of the firm. The six TQM steps are almost self-explanatory; however, they are briefly discussed as they relate to information needs.

Understanding customer requirements is not an automatic activity. It is necessary, first, to generate data periodically and systematically and then generate information by prioritization. As step one leads in the direction of opportunities, identifying problems as well as opportunities from above prioritization provides the firm with the new opportunities as well as the threats (Kotler 1994). These opportunities and threats provide the focus the marketing decision maker needs in establishing the parameters for the firm's marketing plans. Analyzing causes of problems in the marketplace and the way the firm addresses these leads to the development of the details of the marketing plan. This

TQM Steps	Information Status
1. Check customer requirements (what does the customer want?)	1. Both data underload and information underload.
2. Identify problems and opportunities (what is the customer not getting?)	2. Information underload.
3. Analyze causes (what is causing problems?)	3. Special emphasis on both data gathering and information development.
4. Develop plans (brainstorming for ideas for corrective action)	4. Need extra emphasis on special information, however cannot be accomplished without the first 3 steps.
5. Implement improvements (put corrective action to work)	5. Need special information on the marketing plan and its implementation.
6. Monitor results (meet the customers' expectations)	6. Feedback activity for all of the above steps. Decision maker must have instant access to all.

Exhibit 1–6 The Modern Total Quality Management Concept and Information Needs

activity requires extra emphasis on special information. However, it also requires special attention to the first three steps.

Implementing the marketing plans with additional improvements requires additional detailed information so that the decision maker can improve the marketing plans. However, implementation decisions require additional information. Finally, monitoring the results of the total activity is absolutely essential. Unless there is early feedback as to the firm's overall performance, TQM cannot succeed. The marketing decision maker must have instant access to all of this required information. Above all, Exhibits 1–3 and 1–6 imply not only having proper information but also learning how to use it. This implies organizational learning.

ORGANIZATIONAL LEARNING

Market orientation and TQM are important; however, developing an atmosphere of organizational learning is essential for long-term survival in the market place. In Exhibit P–1, two gaps are mentioned: the information gap and the learning gap. Without eliminating the information gap, it is impossible to develop good marketing decisions and implement TQM. However, without eliminating the learning gap, the firm will not have any continuity in its use of information or its implementation of TQM. In this discussion, the elimination of the learning gap is called organizational learning.

Organizational learning has been in the management literature since the late 1970s (Argyris 1991). A basic definition of organizational learning indicates the development of new knowledge or insights that potentially will alter behavior. Here it is implied that the acquisition of meaningful learning requires behavior change. Behavior change, in turn, is the key to organizational improvement. Two more implications must be identified here. First, those firms that can generate new data and acquire new knowledge but are unable to apply it to their own activities are *not* adequately involved in organizational learning. Second, those organizations that allow their behavior to be influenced only indirectly by new knowledge are not involved in organizational learning. Their future performance cannot be improved, and they will not be able to cope with the ever-increasing and ever-changing environment of market turbulence (see Exhibit I–1) (Slater & Narver 1994).

If the learning gap were to be eliminated, which must occur for the firm to succeed in the long run, the organization must have a memory. As Slater and Narver (1994) posited, it is essential that important knowledge in the organization be codified and recorded in specific operating procedures, decision-making situations, mission statements, and the like.

Developing an organizational memory, however, must include developing what some people have called a "competency trap" (Leonard-Barton 1992; Slater & Narver 1994). A competency trap occurs when new procedures or capabilities are better than the old ones but, because of heavy investments or traditionalism, they are rejected. For instance, International Business Machines (IBM) in the 1980s, maintained its focus on, and commitment to, mainframe computers, even though the market was moving in a different direction.

The generation of information and the elimination of learning gaps thus lead to corporate behavior changes. Maintaining the link between knowledge development and learning how to use it effectively is the prime responsibility of the firm's information system (IS). Information leading to learning and, hence, behavior change, implies the need for *understanding* the whole process. The IS must identify an *information responsibility*. It is maintained throughout this book that this responsibility is identified by the marketing decision maker in conjunction with the researchers' input. It is also maintained throughout this book that the information responsibility for marketing decisions must rest on the marketing decision maker. This particular person must understand the evolutionary process in data gathering and information generation, as well as the subsequent behavior changes that are related to further learning through use of the newly developed information.

SUMMARY

Possessing the proper market orientation is not enough for a company to perform well in turbulent markets. In addition, the firm must build a learning organization. This is achieved by developing a well-managed and powerful IS. There is an evolution occurring in information technology. This chapter indicates that EDP, MIS, DSS, and SIS are all specific phases. An attempt is made here to debunk a general misconception and instead to posit that there is currently a general data overload accompanied by an information underload. It is maintained here that the firm must develop a balanced information system (IS). A balanced IS is powerful and leads to the necessary behavior changes to cope with the changing and, perhaps, increasing adversity of the marketplace.

This balance is related to the IS having proper access to both external and internal data. Unless such a balance exists, the firm will not be able to take advantage of both its internal and external opportunities, and without such a balance, the firm cannot optimize its performance.

The next section of the chapter deals with total quality management (TQM). It is maintained that in addition to other counterturbulence activities, the firm can improve its market position through TQM. However, TQM cannot be implemented unless the necessary information is made available to the marketing decision maker.

Finally, eliminating the knowledge gaps is not enough. In addition, the firm must use TQM over a prolonged period of time. This is achieved by having a learning organization and by eliminating the learning gap.

REFERENCES

Alter, Steven L. 1980. *Decision Support Systems*. Reading, MA: Addison-Wesley.
Argyris, Chris. 1991. "Teaching Smart People How to Learn." *Harvard Business Review* (May-June): 99–109.
Arinze, Bay. 1990. "Market Planning with Computer Models: A Case Study in the Software Industry." *Industrial Marketing Management* 19:117–129.
"Banks Find Areas to Trim." 1991. *ABA Banking Journal* (December): 22.
Bessen, Jim. 1993. "Riding the Marketing Information Wave." *Harvard Business Review* (September-October): 151–160.
Cravens, David W. 1982. *Strategic Marketing*. Homewood, IL: Richard D. Irwin.
Gronroos, Christian. 1990. *Service Management and Marketing*. Lexington, MA: Lexington Books.

Kavan, C. Bruce, Cheryl J. Frohlich, and A. Coskun Samli. 1994. "Developing a Balanced Information System." *Journal of Services Marketing* 8(1): 4–13.

Kotler, Philip. 1994. *Marketing Management*. Englewood Cliffs, NJ: Prentice-Hall.

Leonard-Barton, Dorothy. 1992. "Core Capabilities and Core Rigidities: A Paradox in Managing New Product Development." *Strategic Management Journal* 13:111–25.

Mentzer, John T., and Nimish Gandhi. 1992. "Expert Systems in Marketing: Guidelines for Development." *Journal of the Academy of Marketing Science* (Winter): 73–80.

Montgomery, David B., and Charles B. Weinberg. 1979. "Toward Strategic Intelligence Systems." *Journal of Marketing* 41–52.

Naisbitt, John. 1982. *Megatrends*. New York: Warner Books.

"Quality: How to Make it Pay." 1994. *Business Week*, August 8, 54–59.

Samli, A. Coskun. 1985. "International Strategic Information Systems." In *Proceedings*. Miami, FL: Second World Marketing Congress, Academy of Marketing Science.

Samli, A. Coskun, and Cheryl Frohlich. 1992. "Service: The Competitive Edge in Banking." *Journal of Services Marketing* (Winter): 15–22.

Schaderbek, Charles G. 1985. *Management Systems: Conceptual Considerations*. Plano, TX: Business Publications.

Slater, Stanley F., and John C. Narver. 1994. *Market Oriented Isn't Enough: Build a Learning Organization*. Report no. 94–103. Cambridge, MA: Marketing Science Institute.

"Success of AT&T Universal Card Puts Pressure on Big Banks to Reduce Rates." 1992. *Wall Street Journal*, February 4, B-1, col. 3.

"Universal Card Faces Growing Competition." *Florida Times Union*, February 5, d-7, col. 4.

Zeithaml, V., L. L. Berry, and A. Parasuraman. 1988. "Communication and Control Processes in the Delivery of Service Quality." *Journal of Marketing*. (April): 35–48.

The Current Status of American Marketing Research

INTRODUCTION

As Haeckel and Nolan (1993) stated, flexibility and responsiveness rule the marketplace. Of course, this has been the case, not just recently, but since day one. However, if a firm needs to be flexible and responsive to market changes, this does not mean it has to be managed by wire. In other words, sensing and responding to changing customer needs is essential. When these changing needs are detected, the firm must have the information on which to base behavior changes in its marketing. Over the past three decades or more, companies have put much emphasis on information technology. As such, they have generated much data. However, they have not sufficiently emphasized generating information. They have not interpreted, analyzed and made sense out of the data that would enable them to act swiftly and effectively. In short, they did not facilitate the necessary changes in marketing. On the other side of information technology is marketing research. During the same period of time, marketing research became extremely sophisticated in methodology, but not in its application. This leads, in the famous words of Peters (1989), to *paralysis through analysis*. This chapter presents a balanced view of how information technology without marketing sensitivity is wasteful and also how too much marketing research methodology without appropriate information technology becomes totally suboptimal. Above all, this chapter reiterates the point that information development should lead to better marketing decisions. Here, the marketing decision maker has the responsibility for the development and use of the firm's information system (IS).

MANAGING BY WIRE AND MARKETING REALITIES

Haeckel and Nolan (1993) discussed managing by wire by examining jet-engine technology. Instrumentation and communication technologies provide criteria to evaluate alternative responses. Computer systems intercept the pilot's special commands and translate them into thousands of detailed orders. This is how the plane's functions are arranged. Haeckel and Nolan go on to describe the ideal manage-by-wire implementation for a business. They think this system represents the operations of an entire business. Such a model would have all the modern information technologies, such as expert systems, databases, software objects, and other technical components needed to manage by wire.

Haeckel and Nolan (1993, 123) left an important exit avenue by stating:

> Of course, if the enterprise model represents the wrong reality—or is incomplete, out of date, or operating on bad data—the outcome could be catastrophic, like putting engines in reverse at 30,000 feet. Creating a robust model of a large business organization is an extremely challenging undertaking.

However, this is not quite enough. Because of the prevailing tendency to use information technology and computer modeling to arrive at critical business decisions automatically, the art and science of marketing decision making has been going through a process of dehumanization and automation.

Additionally, Watters and Shepherd (1994) posited that information paradigms have traditionally been data-centered. As they stated, "a paradigm provides a framework or model within which specific characteristics and properties of systems can be studied" (455). Traditionally, information systems have been developed in such a way that the data can be used effectively as well as efficiently. For instance, information retrieval systems were created to allow the users access to much unstructured data. Similarly, database management systems were also developed to provide users access to unstructured data. In both cases, data access is developed mainly through exploring languages that reflect the structure of the data, and the user, by using the structure, maps out his or her information need and draws from the database (Watters & Shepherd 1994). In all these cases, the user has to transform the information needed into an exact request that is presented in terms of the data and structure available. This is the traditional data-centered information paradigm, which is based on the basic premise that information needs can be expressed in the forms of exact requests formulated in the language of the system.

Whether the information paradigm is data-centered or user-centered, automated information generation cannot possibly satisfy the information needs of the modern user. Samli (1993, 136) stated, "Because customer needs are becoming more and more individualized and customers are becoming smarter and more discriminating, individualized marketing in the 1990s became a necessity." In such cases, the appropriateness of the marketing message, the quality and customization of the product or service, and the depth of personal relationships with each customer make it totally impossible to use automated data for very specific marketing decisions. Modern American markets are so turbulent and changeable that marketing information cannot be standardized and automated. Rather, it has to be more flexible than the markets themselves, so that decision makers can establish and exercise a competitive advantage based on their company's market-oriented performance. The same reasoning applies to production-related data gathered from batches versus single manufacturing lines. Whereas data from batches are more efficiently gathered and more voluminous, they are not quite of the same quality. Thus, there is a condition of data overload and information underload. On the other hand, single manufacturing lines provide specific, step-by-step information. Hence, data overload and information underload are eliminated. Only in the case of the customization that is required of modern marketing do single manufacturing lines rely on, and provide, good information.

As seen from our discussion thus far, automation, along with the erroneous notion that data are the basis for everything, has created ineffectiveness, indecisiveness, and mistakes in the decision-making process. Of course, marketing research has developed its own frailties as it also pursued automation, databases, and quick decision-making activities.

WHAT IS WRONG WITH THE CURRENT STATUS OF MARKETING RESEARCH?

With the emergence of computers and information technology, two key trends have come to dominate marketing research: (1) methodological advances, (2) generation of as much data as possible without much management input (the data-centered information paradigm).

As can be seen, the information problems in the modern enterprise can be grouped into two layers. First of all, the information system of the firm is taking off in its own way. Second, marketing research is also going in a different direction. Both of these sets of problems are having a critical impact on the ability to make appropriate marketing decisions in the present turbulent markets of the United Stats and, indeed, the world.

Although there will be much discussion of information system problems in this book, the following discussion is related to marketing research problems.

TOO MUCH METHODOLOGY

With the advent of computers during the past two decades, marketing researchers went to work on developing new methodologies to convert data into information. Starting with univariate and bivariate analyses, many new multivariate techniques came into being (see Chapter 10). Analyses moved from simple correlation to multiple regression, multiple discriminant analyses, factor analyses, canonical analyses, and a series of multiattribute techniques. The outcomes were very exciting, and the developing methodology provided some power to marketing researchers. As a result, increasing amounts of effort went into generating new methodologies to manipulate the data.

Although manipulating the data is not a bad premise in itself, over-manipulation of data can be extremely costly, redundant, and particularly misleading. As increasing emphasis was put into generating new techniques and methodologies, the mission of marketing research was lost. The reason for the existence of marketing research is to facilitate the decision-making process. If marketing research becomes an end in itself by simply questing for new and more methodologies, then it loses its mission of being a critical means to an end. Thus, marketing research during the past two decades has become too theoretical and impractical. When marketing research loses its perspectives and cannot fulfill its mission, a firm is likely to make unnecessary and ineffective decisions, which can prove to be very costly. These decisions will never be optimal unless they are based on appropriate information.

TOO LITTLE SUBSTANCE

When methodology becomes the focal point of the total research activity, then much research effort and activity go into testing methodological theories on insignificant samples and, particularly, relatively unimportant topics. Whereas typically, information needs to be satisfied by the data obtained from the most appropriate samples that would represent the firm's markets, in methodology testing, convenience samples such as students are used. Although additional methodological nuances may not contribute to the firm's well-being, they are revered by research methodologists. In the meantime, a void is created between the research activity and the decision process. This is due to having too little substance in the research findings as inadequate access to correctly collected and processed data (i.e., marketing information).

MISSING INFORMATION-DRIVEN DECISION MAKING

In a market economy, the survival and success of a firm depends upon the use of marketing information in its decision-making process (Samli 1993). Our discussion, however, posits that marketing decision makers are not exercising information-driven decision making. Exhibit 2–1 illustrates problems of marketing research in the modern enterprise. In addition to losing its focus, marketing research has started to generate scattered data (Lingle & Schiemann 1994). Data scatter results from the poor job done by organizations in gathering, managing, and transforming data into information systems.

As seen in Exhibit 2–1, data access problems are more critical in the marketing decision-making process. The exhibit is based on a study by Katz (1991), and data access problems are listed on the basis of their relative importance. Poor documentation is the most important data access problem, while staff resistance is the least important data access problem, in comparison with the others. From Exhibit 2–1, it is clear that documentation or programming (including different configurations) creates a major hindrance to data accessibility. This is at least partially related to the suppliers' lack of competence. However, the users also may not be sufficiently well trained to make good use of the data. In the final analysis, the marketing decision maker has to be in a position to sort out the scattered data and establish efficient access. Efficient access in this context means being able to retrieve the specific type of processed data (information) needed for the intended decision area, and to do so as quickly as possible.

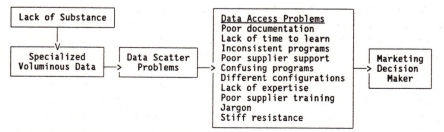

Exhibit 2–1 Marketing Research Problems

It is extremely critical to reiterate that here, decision makers have the main responsibility to decide on their information needs. The same decision maker should not think that decisions can be made automatically, based on some formula. Nor can computers tell decision makers exactly what to do.

Until recently, decision makers have relied on the well-informed researcher. However, the researcher or information system specialist cannot possibly be sensitive enough to tell the decision maker what type of information to use. At the same time, unless decision makers understand the nature and characteristics of information and how it is developed, they will never optimize the information use activity, which is vital to successful decision making. Basically, decision makers must understand the research process and how information is generated. Furthermore, they must be in touch with the research process itself to be able to evaluate the strengths and weaknesses of the information created by the researcher.

Exhibit 2–2 illustrates the research process. If the researcher (or decision maker) does not understand this process, there cannot be sufficient appreciation for information and the decision maker will not be altogether competent to understand the information needs and how they should be used in the decision-making process. The beginning of the process is extremely important in that if the problem is not understood, appropriate data and, subsequently, information cannot be obtained. While the business problem is totally the decision maker's responsibility, translating a business problem into a research problem has to be a joint decision. For instance, General Electric (GE) may be exploring the possibility of introducing a new, more efficient, and more energy-saving microwave oven. The decision of market entry will depend on the researcher's exploration of how the features of the proposed oven will influence the prospective customers, or the market potential for such a product. Exhibit 2-2 illustrates the research process, most of which is the responsibility of the researcher (as opposed to the decision maker). The researcher has to establish objectives for the project. These may involve determining market potentials in specific segments and understanding which features of the proposed appliance are the most desirable. Hypotheses may be formulated on the basis of, say, the upper-middle class in the Northwest, which may be the best market, and which may appear to be more concerned with speed and size than energy efficiency.

Hence, the information needs will relate to the individual's socioeconomic characteristics and willingness to buy a product with certain specifications. Types of information will be more factual and attitudinal. Therefore, this will involve survey research in the proposed market areas, and the participants may be the first-time microwave buyers.

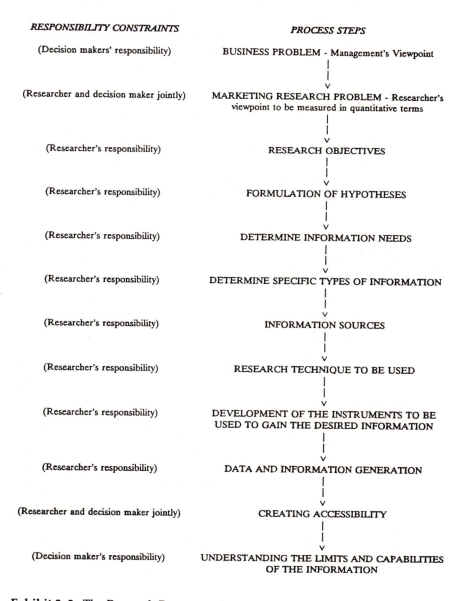

RESPONSIBILITY CONSTRAINTS

(Decision makers' responsibility)

(Researcher and decision maker jointly)

(Researcher's responsibility)

(Researcher's responsibility)

(Researcher's responsibility)

(Researcher's responsibility)

(Researcher's responsibility)

(Researcher's responsibility)

(Researcher's responsibility)

(Researcher's responsibility)

(Researcher and decision maker jointly)

(Decision maker's responsibility)

PROCESS STEPS

BUSINESS PROBLEM - Management's Viewpoint

↓

MARKETING RESEARCH PROBLEM - Researcher's viewpoint to be measured in quantitative terms

↓

RESEARCH OBJECTIVES

↓

FORMULATION OF HYPOTHESES

↓

DETERMINE INFORMATION NEEDS

↓

DETERMINE SPECIFIC TYPES OF INFORMATION

↓

INFORMATION SOURCES

↓

RESEARCH TECHNIQUE TO BE USED

↓

DEVELOPMENT OF THE INSTRUMENTS TO BE USED TO GAIN THE DESIRED INFORMATION

↓

DATA AND INFORMATION GENERATION

↓

CREATING ACCESSIBILITY

↓

UNDERSTANDING THE LIMITS AND CAPABILITIES OF THE INFORMATION

Exhibit 2–2 The Research Process and Shared Responsibilities

The researcher at this point needs to develop the questionnaires, observation forms, and so forth in order to gather the appropriate data. The types of analyses used to test the hypotheses will determine how the data will become information. At this point, the researcher and the decision maker will decide jointly on the format and availability of the research findings. Finally, the decision maker must have the capability to see the strengths and weaknesses of the study and its implications for the development of a marketing plan or abandonment of the project completely.

Having explored the relative responsibilities of both parties (researchers and decision makers), it must be understood that in recent years, because of confusion in these responsibilities, *data overload* (or data scatter) has become a widespread reality. Commensurate to the data overload is *information underload*. Market risks necessitate making information-based decisions. If information underload is a reality, then by definition, businesses are not capitalizing on their market opportunities, thus increasing the risk factors they face.

INFORMATION UNDERLOAD AND EFFECTIVE MARKETING

In recent years, American firms have gone overboard in the cost reduction area (Samli 1992). Instead of enhancing market sensitivity and trying to understand their customers' needs, wants, preferences, and frustrations, the firms have relied increasingly on cost reduction. This situation has brought about major problems for the firms in their competitive skills. The same movement has led to the emergence of total quality management (TQM) because of the glaring shortfalls of the overly cost-oriented firm's performance in the marketplace.

As marketing decisions were made within the cost constraints, they became rather dehumanized. Firms kept on cutting down the marketing- and service-related costs. Automated decision making via computers worsened the conditions. The firms became less competitive and, hence, instead of dealing with marketing tools to cope with market forces, they opted to buy out their competition (Samli 1993).

Perhaps two lessons may be learned from these experiences: (1) Computers do not generate information, they simply generate scattered data. Therefore, they cannot be relied on to make final and critical marketing decisions. (2) Computers cannot make decisions. They simply do not have the vision or capability to understand the ever-changing market conditions.

NEEDED: A USER-CENTERED
INFORMATION PARADIGM

It is believed that the problems discussed in the previous section are creating a paradigm shift from data-centered to decision maker–centered systems. As seen in the information generation stage of Exhibit 2–2, users (or decision makers) often cannot articulate their exact information needs. There have been attempts to develop systems "that can capture and respond to the rather amorphous information needs of users" (Watters & Shepherd 1994, 456). Other attempts are also in place to eliminate access and language barriers between the decision maker and the information base. In the final analysis, only the decision maker can truly recognize if and when the information need has been satisfied (the last step in Exhibit 2–2). However, when the decision maker is ready and the information needs are not satisfied, only disaster awaits the firm in the marketplace.

The user-centered information paradigm is closely connected to the level of market knowledge. This is the level of sophistication in generating, understanding, and using data and information by the individual firm as a whole or by marketing decision makers, specifically in the firm. There exists a hierarchy of market knowledge, and different firms and decision makers are positioned at different levels of this hierarchy. User-centered information systems are likely to shape the basis of the knowledge level that prevails in the firm, as depicted by the firm's researchers and decision makers (Sinkula 1994). Sinkula (1994) referred to levels of market knowledge concept as organizational learning. In our case, it is necessary to discuss specifically the market knowledge levels that prevail on the part of researchers and decision makers.

Exhibit 2–3 illustrates a seven-level market knowledge hierarchy. At the dictionary stage, basic data systems reflect the most common facts about the market. They include market segment definitions and sales activity of different products. The episodic level implies recent trends. Descriptions of past sales and past causal sales are parts of this level. Historic databases indicate somewhat more than simple data; they indicate that the research is attempting to explain what has been happening in the recent past.

The endorsed level indicates the desired level of activities, market performance, and other competitive posture. Market research activity attempts to establish the desired level of performance in the market place. Research is both exploratory and confirmatory. The procedural level explains how things are done. Researchers and decision makers both give greater attention to confirmatory research. This is the research that has been going on and, although not quite routinized, is necessary.

Knowledge Level	The Key Question	Responsibility*	Manifestation	Illustration	Research Activity
Dictionary	"What is?"	R	Definitions of things, labels, & events.	Description of market segments, product movement, & market semantics.	Standard data generation.
Episodic	"What has been?"	R	Value is placed in the development of historical data bases.	Description of past sales, past causal relationships, & phenomena.	Sophisticated analyses of data.
Endorsed	"What is the desired way of doing things?"	R&D	An organizational system of norms, assumptions, & strategies is developed.	When market research information is interpreted the desired performance is to view both exploratory and confirmatory research with equal objectivity.	Standard data and some information.
Procedural	"How things are *actually* done?"	R&D	A task system governed by tacit rules develops among members which may vary from the *espoused* system.	Researchers and decision makers actually give greater attention to confirmatory research and avoid research which contains too many surprises.	Joint effort to generate information.
Axiomatic	"Why things are done the way they are?"	D	Fundamental beliefs appear as organizational values which are set *a priori* and cannot be further reduced.	Over time and perhaps unnecessarily, market research continues to acquire information because the organization takes stock in the marketing concept and considers itself "information driven."	Data and information requirements.
Augmented	"How *should* things be done?"	D	Response to detected differences between the *espoused* vs. the *actual* way of doing things takes the form of joint inquiry into organizational norms themselves so as to resolve inconsistency and create new norms.	Market research joins with brand managers to conduct analyses which result in the decentralization of the market research function.	Requirements of decision specific information.
Deutero	"How does the organization create knowledge and learn?"	R&D	The organization's members learn about organizational learning.	Market research, brand managers, and others examine the impact of organizational structure changes on the knowledge creation process in the firm.	Growth and maturity in information generation.

*R = Researcher; D = Decision-maker; R&D = Joint responsibility   Source: Adopted and revised from Sinkula (1994).

Exhibit 2–3   The Market Knowledge Hierarchy

The axiomatic level indicates the ability to explain reasons behind the events, activities, or market facts. Certain information is generated because the decision makers believe that market orientation requires it. The augmented level takes the exploration activity one step further. Data are gathered with the question in mind: "How should things be done?" Here, serious information needs to be generated to establish the opportunities for the firm as opposed to threats that it is facing. Here, the movement from data to information is very critical. Unless the data are converted into information, this level of sophistication cannot be achieved. It must be noted that almost all the critical decisions are specified by the decision maker. Thus, unless the decision maker understands the research needs and evaluates the importance of additional information, this level in the spectrum cannot be achieved.

The deutero level is the most advanced stage in developing and using market knowledge for the decision-making process. The way in which information is created in the company and how the learning and knowledge take place so that researchers can generate the necessary information for the decision makers are all described by the word *deutero*, which means that constant learning needs to be cultivated so that the firm's performance will continually improve.

During the past two decades or so, with the tendency toward automating data generation and decision making, most American firms have not gone beyond the "procedural" level. Unless the joint effort of researchers and decision makers does take the firm beyond this level, as markets become more turbulent, the risk factor will grow. The firm will simply be unable to capitalize on the market opportunities that it faces.

SUMMARY

This chapter presents a rather gloomy picture of the status of current American marketing research. It points out that, first, marketing research is increasingly being outranked by computerized and automated data generation and, second, it is being weakened by an undue emphasis on methodology. The situation has created a data overload and an information underload.

It is posited here that there should be no gap between the researcher and the decision maker. Of course, the decision maker must understand how the research process generates information so that sound, information-based decisions can be made. In this light, it is proposed in this chapter that there is (or there should be) a paradigm shift from data-centered to user-centered systems. While the former does generate data and/or information of sorts, the latter generates information for the user, who happens to be the decision maker. A seven-level hierarchy of market knowledge is presented in an effort to explain the relationship between researchers and decision makers. User-centered information systems depend on the users' level of sophistication. Unless they know what they need and what needs to be done, the market responsiveness of the firm will be diminished.

REFERENCES

Haeckel, Stephen H., and Richard L. Nolan. 1993. "Managing by Wire." *Harvard Business Review* (September-October): 122–32.

Katz, Helen. 1991. "How Major U.S. Advertising Agencies are Coping with Data Overload." *Journal of Advertising Research* (March): 7–16.

Lingle, John H., and William A. Schiemann. 1994. *Management Review* (May): 53–56.

Peters, Tom. 1989. *Thriving on Chaos*. New York: Alfred A. Knopf.

Samli, A. Coskun. 1992. *Social Responsibility in Marketing*. Westport, CT: Quorum Books.

———. *Counterturbulence Marketing*. Westport, CT: Quorum Books.

Sinkula, James M. 1994. "Market Information Processing and Organizational Learning." *Journal of Marketing* (January): 35–45.

Watters, Carolyn, and Michael A. Shepherd. 1994. "Shifting the Information Paradigm from Data-Centered to User-Centered." *Information Processing and Management* 30(4): 455–471.

3

What Decision Makers Should Know about Information

INTRODUCTION

If the key marketing decisions require information, and if there exits a data overload but an information underload, decision makers need to make many decisions about data and information before they can reach marketing decisions. Three groups of activities need to be understood by the decision maker: (1) how data are generated, (2) how information is created, and (3) how the quality of information is assessed. This chapter deals with all three areas. It first explores different ways of data gathering. Second, it presents a discussion on data processing and information generation. Finally, the chapter discusses the process of quality assessment of information.

Unless he or she can understand the quality, or lack thereof, of the information generated, the decision maker cannot possibly discriminate among different sets of information. One of the key prerequisites of becoming a good decision maker is to understand and use the available information in the decision process. All available information is not of the same quality; therefore, the decision maker has to be discriminating in understanding, selecting, and using information. Exhibit 3–1 illustrates the relationship among the three key components of this chapter. The exhibit also goes on to connect these three components to changing marketing practices. This is what is meant by a learning organization that leads to behavior change. However, this point is discussed in various other chapters (Chapters 1, 12, and 13).

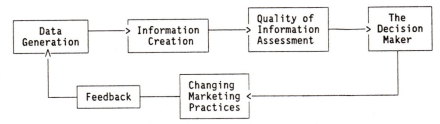

Exhibit 3–1   Information Development

DATA GENERATION

In order to develop an effective marketing information system (IS), Exhibit 3–1 must be carefully studied. There are at least five key ways of collecting or generating data. These are asking direct and indirect questions (surveys); observing the behavior of people (observation); experimenting with different variables and ascertaining their impact on people; extrapolating or interpolating existing data (inferences); and generating additional data by computers based on certain simulation procedures.

Thus, in generating data there are critical decisions to be made as to whether data should be gathered through direct contact with subjects, without being involved, by using computers, by a complicated manipulation of variables, or simply by expanding existing data. These different approaches to data generation do not yield the same results; each has its place and specific features. Marketing decision makers must not only understand the strengths and weaknesses of these approaches but also know how the data that are being considered were gathered.

DATA GENERATION TECHNIQUES

Exhibit 3–2 displays some of the key features of the major data-gathering (and -generating) techniques. Five general techniques are presented in the exhibit: (1) direct contact, (2) using computers, (3) manipulation of variables, (4) expanding existing data, and (5) noninvolvement.

The direct contact techniques are surveys. There are a number of them, and each has unique features. However, in general terms, surveys are very versatile. They can be long or short or use various forms, and they can satisfy different needs of data collection. They can easily obtain detailed and desirable data. However, they are time-consuming and quite costly. The cost factor first stems from the fact that many field

Technique	Features
Direct Contact	Versatile, easier to obtain detailed data, more time consuming, costly, numerous response problems, takes longer to convert to knowledge.
Using Computers	Various simulation models are based on limited data base and different techniques of generating random data. Easier to obtain, more limited use.
Manipulation of Variables	Experimentation is very costly and difficult in social situations and markets. More modern computerized experimentation models are complex and still costly. But the data are definitive.
Expanding Existing Data	Inferences extrapolation and interpolation all require a very good data base and high level statistical and research skills. In some cases this technique is absolutely necessary. Can be reasonable in terms of application and not too costly.
Without Being Involved	Observation is the least costly data gathering technique. Unique and appropriate data can be gathered quickly and efficiently.

Exhibit 3–2 Important Features of Different Data Generation Techniques

workers are needed to undertake a survey. Also, in many cases, specialists are needed to develop instruments and interpret the data gathered. Similarly, survey data take longer to be converted into knowledge.

Gathering data without being involved is called observation. This technique is perhaps the least costly and most misunderstood data-gathering approach. It can generate some very unique and timely data that are appropriate for the problem on hand. With observation, data can be gathered very quickly and efficiently. It does not require a large number of field workers and specialists.

Using computers to generate data typically implies the use of simulation. There are a number of simulation models, which can generate a large variety of data. However, simulations are not very effective unless they have the proper basic parameters on which the data generation can be undertaken. They may require some basic survey data or some other basic key assumptions or models so that the generated data are useful. The data usually have limited use but are quite easy to obtain.

Manipulating variables and determining the impact of these manipulations is called experimentation. Experimentation is costly and difficult because, particularly in social settings and in marketing, there are too many variables for which to account. Thus, trying to identify the impact of a manipulated variable is very difficult. However, experiments yield definitive results concerning the factors behind the event and causality. In recent years, however, more modern computerized experimentation models have generated important data and some invaluable information. Causality in marketing, if it can be established, is extremely important, since marketing plans are based on variables with expected significant impacts. For instance, questions such as "What is the expected impact of 20 percent increased advertising efforts?" or "What would be the market's reaction to a 10 percent decrease in the firm's price structure?" can be answered by experimentation.

Expanding existing data involves generating new data through inferences or developing trend analysis based on time series or other past data. This is a process partially of generating new data and partially of creating information. In both cases, in addition to a very good quality and variety of past data, high-level statistical and research skills are essential. This is partially the "augmented" level of the marketing knowledge hierarchy. These various data collection (or generation) techniques are discussed in Chapter 2 and throughout this book.

TYPES OF DATA AND CONVERSION INTO INFORMATION

Marketing decisions depend on good data. The data are converted into information, and the information is utilized for marketing decisions. As these decisions create a certain impact, knowledge, which is based on learning and experience, emerges. Thus, the decision maker must understand research in order to appreciate data and information as critical inputs for decision making.

Three types of data need to be identified, all of which are very critical for the marketing decision maker: (1) facts, (2) attitudes, and (3) motives. These also are discussed in different sections of this book. However, a brief discussion is necessary here to connect information generation to the assessment of the quality of information.

FACTS

Data bits such as, "people in the XYZ neighborhood go to the grocery store three times a week," or, "people in ABC, on the average, consume 2 gallons of ice cream per month," are facts. Some of the facts are extremely critical for the well-being of the business. Unless these data are gathered and certain facts are known, it may be extremely difficult for the firm to develop and implement an effective marketing plan. Any survey or observation attempt will generate certain facts. However, the researcher must know what specific facts the company needs and, of course, the decision maker must know that, first, these facts are available, and second, there are certain ways of using them. *Webster's Dictionary* (1980, 501) defines a fact as "a thing that has actually happened or that is really true, a thing that has been or is, or the state of things as they are." As can be seen, facts are primarily obtained by surveys or observations. They can be used in conjunction with the firm's understanding or estimates of markets. Understanding or estimating markets will enable the firm to develop and implement effective marketing plans. Consider the following hypothetical facts:

- Suppose that 75 percent of the company's customers watch the daily newscast on a particular network.
- The typical customer spends, on the average, $10 per week for the company's products.
- The company's customers are primarily young adults living in upscale suburbs who own their own homes, have one young child, and have a higher-than-national-average education. They shop in shopping centers and supermarkets within a two-mile radius from home.
- Customer brand loyalty is noticeable—80 percent of the company's customers prefer the company's brands over those of competitors.

As can be seen, such information will facilitate the development of new products, advertising campaigns, distribution systems, pricing policies, and above all, effective marketing plans that will enhance the firm's competitive edge. Data that are processed in terms of the firm's needs generate facts (or factual information) that are essential for its marketing performance. In recent years, with advanced technology, on-line databases have been developed, which provide factual data that can be converted into information easily. Similarly, data are gathered through electronic mail (Pearl 1993). In some cases, the outside research groups are trying to adjust the data to the firm's needs and, hence, attempting to generate useful information. At the Nielsen Advanced Information Technology Center, there has been an attempt to help Nielsen survey clients turn data into information that can be used to solve their unique business problems (Wood 1990). However, these efforts are rather costly (Alderson 1993). Nonetheless, these technological advances are increasing the decision maker's options. Here, both the decision maker and researcher must decide the extent to which a set of factual data are more important than other sets of data and, perhaps, some information that is provided by the outside source. While the general technological background of researchers needs to be developed further, the understanding of the marketing decision maker also becomes very critical. In developing a good information system, the decision maker always has to trade off between quality and quantity of the data versus the cost of the data.

Obviously, factual databases are extremely critical for information system (IS) development and, subsequently, for marketing decision makers. However, it must also be reiterated that attitudes and motives are equally important for marketing decision makers.

ATTITUDES

An attitude is a mental state that predisposes the individual to respond in a certain way when subjected to a specific stimulus. Particular experiences of individual consumers, their discussions with others, and their exposure to media influence the formation and modification of attitudes. Clearly, the marketing decision maker would like to see a very positive attitude toward the company name and brands. Thus, it is necessary to, first, determine the customers' (and prospective customers') attitude toward the firm and its product, and then, try to manipulate this attitude in favor of the firm. We must understand that attitudes not only have direction (either away from or, preferably, toward the company's products and brands), but also a certain level of intensity provides strength in that direction. Determining an increase or decrease in that level of intensity is an early indicator as to how the firm is performing in the marketplace. Attitudes are generally viewed as having three components: cognitive knowledge, affective liking, and behavioral (action).

Cognitive refers to our knowledge or beliefs in regard to an object (or the firm or its products).

Affective refers to our negative or positive feelings in regard to an object (or the firm or its products).

Behavioral refers to our predisposition toward action in a given situation (toward the firm and its products or its brands).

Attitudes are measured by scales, which provide respondents with a set of numbered options that represent the range of possible judgments or intensity of these judgments. These are discussed in Chapter 8.

It must be reiterated that marketing decision makers not only need more attitudinal data but also must convert these data into information such as, "our firm's products are preferred two-to-one over those of our major competitor," or, "our customers' like [or dislike] for our company has declined by 25 percent since last year." This type of information provides a clear-cut direction for marketing decisions (Brown 1980;

Aaker and Day 1990). Again, chapter 8 delves into many aspects of this phenomenon.

MOTIVES

Consumers, buyers, shoppers, or any target of questioning may not know the answer to a question. Alternatively, the respondent may not be willing to answer the question or may not consciously know the answer. Marketing has much to learn from the subconscious awareness of certain consumers. This is explored by motivation research. Motives are not consciously clear to the individual and do not surface in typical questioning on a standard questionnaire. Instead, a number of techniques are used to elicit the nature of motives in the consumer's subconscious. These are discussed in Chapter 9. Even if the consumer has no answer to a question, when a motivational research technique is utilized, a deeper and unexpected response will surface. Thus, motives are the root causes behind actions. Once they are understood, the reason behind certain behaviors will be explained.

HOW INFORMATION IS GENERATED

The following is an example of how information is generated. A computer system at Whirlpool Corporation raised a warning flag. There appeared to be a problem with a brand new washing machine model. It appeared that after just a few washloads, the machines were starting to leak badly. As soon as Whirlpool engineers determined the cause (a faulty hose clamp), manufacturing was stopped. The company's computer helped identify each of the few hundred customers who had purchased the machines so that the washers could be repaired. Thus, from general data about product performance, customer services at Whirlpool developed specific information to keep customers happy (*Business Week* March 21, 1994).

However, until recently, knowing your own customers was not easy. Computer technology was not up to the job. The data existed but were too voluminous, too widely scattered throughout the organization, and not recorded consistently enough to provide support for important marketing decisions (*Business Week* March 21, 1994). This is the fine line that distinguishes data from information. Unless properly gathered, organized, processed, analyzed, and delivered, data are not information. These functions are critical stages of marketing research and are discussed throughout this book. Here, only properly gathered, organized, and processed aspects of the data are associated with information.

Criteria for Information Generation	Implications
Relationship	The data must be closely related to the firm.
Priority	The data must deal with most important information priority.
Quality	The information must be of high quality.
Decisions	The information must lead to specific marketing decisions.
Completeness	The information must be complete.
Follow-up	At the decision point there should not be need for additional information.

Exhibit 3–3 From Data to Information

The decision maker must be in a position to determine if the data that are being accessed will be good enough information for the decision-making process. Exhibit 3–3 presents six basic criteria that would indicate that the data are converted into good information for decision making. These criteria are: (1) relationship, (2) priority, (3) quality, (4) decisions, (5) completeness, and (6) follow-up.

Relationship

The data may show that in the cities X, Y, and Z, consumers spend about 20 percent of their income on groceries. However, this does not quite provide information for the marketing decision maker of, say, the high-status Florida grocery chain, Publix. If the customers of Publix were to be extracted from the data (thus providing information for Publix), it may show that they spend only 15 percent of their income on groceries and buy quite different groups of products than average consumers. Without such knowledge, Publix may advertise to the wrong people, plan its inventories incorrectly, and offer a merchandise mix that is less than optimal.

Thus, the marketing decision maker must make sure that the original data have been converted into information that is very pertinent to the firm. The relationship between data and the firm indicates if these data will be converted into information.

General Data	Publix Information
Four brands account for 40% Brand A accounts for 25% Brand B accounts for 10%	Four brands account for 45% Brand A accounts for 15% Brand B accounts for 30%

Exhibit 3–4   General Data versus Publix Information

Priority

There are always plenty of data; however, the marketing decision maker must ensure that the data used for the decision-making process are the most important for the firm. In other words, the decision maker should be able to sort through the data, single out the most important information for the firm, and use this information. Exhibit 3–4 illustrates this point. When data are converted to meet Publix's needs, information is generated. Here the priority is brand B.

Obviously, brand B is extremely important for Publix. The information presented in Exhibit 3–4 indicates that Publix customers are different from the average and have very strong preferences. This information, once again, provides a basis for advertising, inventory control, and merchandise mix decisions. In this case, it is the highest-priority information.

Quality

Although the researcher must generate good data, in the final analysis, the decision maker is responsible for the data's quality. Just what are the criteria for good data? There are at least six that need to be considered: (1) reliability, (2) validity, (3) sensitivity, (4) relevance, (5) versatility, and (6) ease of response (Luck and Rubin 1987).

Reliability means that the data were produced in such a way that if the study were to be replicated by using the same techniques, the same results will be obtained. That means that the data are not loaded with random errors that make them undependable.

Validity indicates that the data show what they are supposed to show. In other words, the research instrument has measured what it was supposed to measure. Sensitivity implies that the data indicate small changes and variations in the phenomenon that is being represented (or measured) by the data. When the data lack sensitivity, research will not yield significant results and the efforts will be wasted.

Relevance means that the problem to be solved or the decision to be made is practical and important. The data that are gathered will be able to accomplish what they were supposed to do, meaning that the proper data were collected. Versatility indicates robustness. In other words, the data can be used for various statistical analyses. Measuring the phenomenon for various interpretations is made possible if the data are versatile.

Ensuring ease of response on the part of the respondents is always critical. If the questions were difficult or the conditions unsuitable, the data that are gathered may not be good enough. Forcing the respondents to answer in certain ways and not providing enough alternatives in the answer section will result in a lack of ease of response. It is critical that the decision maker can decide on the quality of the data. If the quality is not acceptable, the data can never become information or be used effectively for decision making.

Decisions

The information must lead to effective marketing decision making. Much of the time, information that was converted from data must be very specific so that it will cater to the specificity of the marketing decision area. For instance, if the decision maker is considering a price change decision, it is necessary for the data to approximate demand elasticity and other information to indicate what might be expected as a result of this pricing decision.

Completeness

It is obvious that the information needs to be quite complete. Referring back to Exhibit 3–4, if brand B is very critical for Publix, it is important to know the socioeconomic and demographic characteristics of those who are so loyal to that brand. If the information is not complete, Publix will not know which market niche needs to be reached through special advertising to promote brand B.

Follow-up

Continuing with the concept of completeness, if the data do not provide the necessary information, the decision maker will be put in a difficult position. Making a decision based on incomplete information is dangerous. Again, following the previous example, if we know that brand B is very important for Publix but we do not know the respondents' characteristics or who they are, we cannot direct our promotional activities toward them. If Publix were to promote blindly without knowing exactly what its target markets are, the chances are that it will waste large sums of advertising dollars. It behooves the marketing decision maker to determine if the data have gaps or the information is not complete and what additional information is needed. Thus, the decision maker has to initiate the follow-up activity by requesting additional information.

SUMMARY

This chapter dwells on three key topics: data generation, information creation, and information evaluation.

Five general modes of orientation toward data generation are discussed. These are (1) direct contact, (2) using computers, (3) manipulation of variables, (4) expanding existing data, and (5) noninvolvement. These modes are briefly discussed from the perspective of a marketing decision maker.

Three basic types of data were discussed in this chapter: (1) facts, (2) attitudes, and (3) motives. All these are converted into information; otherwise they are not adequate enough for decision making. The conversion of data into information is the responsibility of marketing researchers. However, the marketing decision maker must evaluate the information to determine whether it is suitable for decision making. Here, the decision maker can use at least six criteria: (1) relationship, (2) priority, (3) quality, (4) decisions, (5) completeness, and (6) follow-up.

REFERENCES

Aaker, David A., and George S. Day. 1990. *Marketing Research*. New York: John Wiley and Sons.
Alderson, Pat. 1993. "Managing the Costs of On-Line Information." *Best's Review*, July, 74–78.
Brown, Francis E. 1980. *Marketing Research*. Reading, MA: Addison-Wesley.
"The Gold Mine of Data in Customer Services." 1994. *Business Week*, March 21, 113–14.
Luck, David J., and Ronald S. Rubin. 1987. *Marketing Research*. Englewood Cliffs, NJ: Prentice-Hall.
Pearl, Jayne A. 1993. "The E-mail Quandary." *Management Review*, July, 48–51.
Webster's New World Dictionary of the American Language. 1980. 2nd College ed.
Wood, Wally. 1990. "Tools of Trade: Packaged Facts." *Marketing and Media Decisions*, July, 60–61.

4

Factual Information in Marketing: Internal

INTRODUCTION

All firms—small, large, or gigantic—have huge internal databases and volumes of internal information. However, much of the internal data are accumulated for non-marketing purposes, and only a very small proportion (if any at all) of these data are converted into marketing information for critical corporate decisions. If the decision maker is not aware of the nature and value of the marketing information that can be generated and successfully used, marketing information will never materialize. Hence, good marketing plans cannot be developed. This situation presents potentially substantial losses in the performance of the firm. Perhaps a worse scenario is that accounting data will be used by accountants to impact the marketing activities of the firm. This chapter presents a systematic approach to analyzing the data overload that many firms constantly experience and remedying information underload by generating valuable marketing information.

ACCOUNTING DATA: A GOLD MINE

The American accounting system is very advanced. All businesses, small and large, have computers that generate valuable data. However, this particular gold mine is not used primarily for marketing decision making. In fact, most of the accounting systems are designed for cost and tax purposes, neither of which can make much contribution to marketing knowledge. However, this gold mine can be converted to significant and extremely valuable marketing information. The fact that the existing accounting data can also be usable to marketing decision makers is an extremely critical bit of information. Once again, the marketing executive must understand the value of this internal data and what kind of information should be extracted from them. Internal accounting data, however, are used more readily by company controllers to impact marketing decisions.

Controllers in corporate entities have reported having important inputs into certain marketing activities. For example, controllers have major input into product costing (Fane 1992). This can be a very important contribution if the proper orientation is used. Assume, for instance, a company with two major product lines. In both cases, fixed and variable costs are taken care of. The company then develops a third product line, the addition of which will be very beneficial to the overall competitive advantage of the firm. Because of the fact that there is excess capacity, the addition of the new product line will not make a significant difference in the fixed cost area. However, if the controller insists that the fixed cost must be allocated proportionately, the new product line may become very costly to consider and market. Thus, product costing from a marketing versus an accounting perspective may be quite different—and critical.

Controllers also report their strong input into corporate marketing audits. Just as in the case discussed above, an accounting orientation to an audit is quite different from a marketing audit. While the accounting audit is more internal and cost-oriented, marketing audits need to be more external and revenue-oriented. Without such marketing audits, it is impossible to identify and capitalize on market opportunities. Controllers' input in sales budgeting also goes in the same direction. If the budget is bottom-line oriented from the beginning and tries to cut costs up front, many sales opportunities will remain unmaterialized.

Controllers have also described their substantial input into product pricing and marketing expense budgeting (Fane 1992). As discussed in regard to product costs, product pricing from an accounting perspective is likely to be cost-oriented. However, marketing-oriented pricing is more likely to be demand-oriented. The latter is likely to yield greater profits to the company.

Finally, perhaps the worst way of using accounting information by accountants to impact marketing activity is via input into marketing expense budgeting. The accounting orientation is strongly cost-related, whereas marketing budgets need to be based on opportunities and revenues.

Exhibit 4–1 illustrates how the gold mine of internal data can (and should) be used. Assuming a good internal data-gathering system, internal data can provide a basis for analyzing all marketing activities as a whole as well as individually. More discussion of this concept is

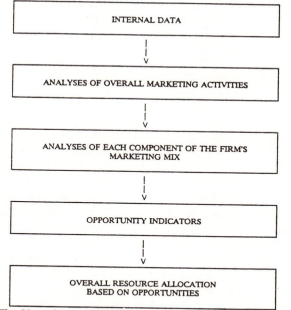

Exhibit 4–1 The Use of Internal Data

presented in Chapter 13. Suffice it here to say that good internal data provide an indication as to how the firm is doing in comparison with past years as well as industry averages and specific competitors (if some of their data are available from secondary sources such as company annual reports). The proper use of internal data is opportunity-, and not necessarily cost-, based. Marketing decision makers must be better informed and trained to use this information in such a way that the existing opportunities can be carefully assessed before the firm's resources are allocated.

If there is a past trend of sales, profits, or return on equity, and if the past year's results are either below or above this trend, this is an indication of the overall performance. This can be dissected into analyses of specific marketing activities, a process that may identify the opportunity areas that need to be emphasized.

Exhibit 4–2 illustrates a hypothetical situation involving a chain of apparel stores. During the 1990–1991 recession, the performance of XYZ apparel chain yielded no profit. In order to not lose money, the chain had to increase its advertising activity by 8 percent; also, its sales showed an increase of 6 percent. This implies either that during the recession, the chain changed its merchandise mix and sold more of

YEAR	TOTAL SALES	ADVERTISING	NET PROFIT
1990-1991	+6%	+8%	0
Industry Average	-12%	-10%	-15

Exhibit 4–2   Performance of XYZ Apparel Chain

low-price and low–mark-up lines, or it lowered its overall price lines and sold more than the previous year without making any money. However, that it held its own in this case may be quite significant. When XYZ's performance is compared with that of the industry on the average, it becomes clear that XYZ has done quite well, as the average industry sales were down by 12 percent. The industry as a whole, unlike XYZ, was trying to cut costs and reduced advertising by 10 percent. The result for the industry as a whole was detrimental, since negative profits were experienced by the average firm in the industry. As can be seen, the analysis of the firm's overall performance indicates important marketing leads, which should be followed carefully. It must be understood here that the firm's overall performance is the outcome of its total resource allocation and use.

Internal data indicating the overall performance of the firm can be dissected in such a way as to evaluate the performance of each element of the marketing mix: product, place, price, and promotion (the "4 Ps"). An evaluation of the firm's products is the first step in this effort.

PRODUCT EVALUATION

All products are not the same in terms of their need-satisfaction features or their contribution to the profit picture. This is why the Boston Consulting Group (BCG) has developed a classification system using the terms, *stars, cash cows, question marks*, and *dogs* (Kotler 1994).

Assume that a company has many products. Companies such as Johnson and Johnson and Procter and Gamble have hundreds of products, each of which has a different performance level and contributes differently to the profit picture. Exhibit 4–3 provides a model to evaluate product performance by using internal accounting data. The performance of each product implies total sales, increased or decreased rate of total sales, costs for promotion, distribution, production, and the like. Once these analyses have been completed, the profit contribution of each product can be determined.

However, at this point, another major area needs to be considered. Some products may be considered as a contributor to the overall profit

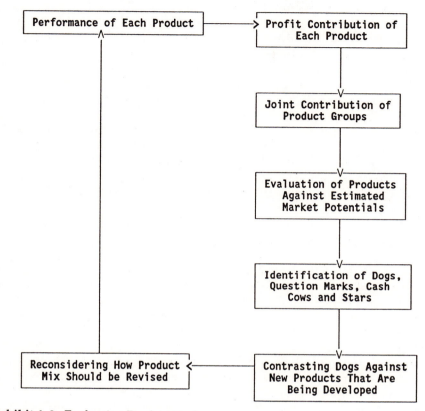

Exhibit 4–3 Evaluating Product Performance

picture only in conjunction with other products. A simple example will illustrate: A large drug store in a southeastern university town has always had a very busy lunch counter. One day, however, the lunch counter has to be closed down because of insufficient revenues. However, the existing data used for this decision did not provide the necessary additional information about the contribution of the lunch crowd to total sales. Most of those who ate lunch also purchased a number of products. Thus, without this information, it was premature to close down the lunch counter. (In many retail stores, loss leaders play such a role.)

Thus, the joint contribution of product groups needs to be assessed rather than the individual product contributions. The latter needs to be adjusted with the input from the former. Once the product contribution has been established, products need to be evaluated on the basis of estimated market potentials. Internal data can provide for only a small aspect of this concept, as they show the growth rates of individual products. Of course, additional market research is needed to determine the market potential for each product. Thus, the internal data cannot accomplish this task alone. (This does not reduce its value.)

If the internal data are supplemented by additional market research inputs as to the market potentials, as in Exhibit 4–3, it becomes possible to identify dogs, question marks, cash cows, and stars. On the basis of this classification, a decision can be made as to which products need to be supported further and which need to be phased out. Here again, additional marketing research inputs are needed to contrast the questionable products with newly proposed ones. However, once this has been accomplished, the firm will be in a position to optimize its product mix.

SALES FORCE ALLOCATION

Product mix is one of the specific areas explored through internal data, and there are numerous other areas that are necessarily evaluated on the basis of internal data. Sales force allocation is one of these critical areas. There are at least two types of evaluation of the sales force made possible by internal data. The first is the overall allocation of the sales effort. Exhibit 4–4 illustrates this phenomenon. A company with multiple markets is not likely to receive the same return for each personal selling dollar in all markets. Exhibit 4–4 illustrates that the return in market A is much greater than in either markets B or C. The critical concept here is that until the return per personal selling dollar is the same in all three markets, there is room for improvement. This improvement will come about, all things being the same, by a reallocation of the sales effort. Clearly, by taking away the sales effort from A and putting it into C, the situation will be improved. By perhaps slightly overcrowding C, the return per sales dollar may go down to $90 in A, but the return in C may climb up to $45. This is because in A, the sales effort becomes more scarce and more selective. The process may continue on the basis of the reaction in C. There may be a point where the return to all three may level off at $75. This would be the optimum result for XYZ company. A reader may ask the question, "Just what is good about the return

XYZ Company Markets	Return on Per Personal Selling Dollar
A	100
B	50
C	15

Exhibit 4–4 Sales Force Allocation Illustration

Performance Index*

Smith	98
Jones	65
Windmeyer	120
Woo	105
Wilkinson	112

*$\dfrac{\text{Actual Sales}}{\text{Sales Quota}}$ X 100

Exhibit 4–5 Evaluation of Each Salesperson

in A going down from $100 to $75?" This decline is compensated richly by the increased volume in all three markets. Also, the reader must consider the increase from $15 to $75 in C and from $50 to $75 in B. In all cases, the volume and total revenue will increase substantially, which will translate into greater profits.

The second aspect of sales force allocation based on internal data is the salespeople's performance evaluation. Exhibits 4–5, 4–6, and 4–7 illustrate this very important concept. If one examines the internal data-based performance index of the five salespeople, it becomes clear that Jones is not performing well. Certainly, the first impression here is that this can be remedied by firing Jones. However, internal data provide additional facts about the situation. Exhibit 4–6 indicates that sound systems produced by the company have not done very well across the country, and have done particularly badly in the company's western markets. Two salespeople, Jones and Woo, cover the West Coast. Exhibit 4–7 compares the performance of these two salespeople. As can be seen, both have had a difficult time selling sound systems. However, further analyses would indicate that Jones was given an unusually large sales quota for sound systems. When the product did

| | Performance Index of Product Lines in Different Regions | | | |
	West	East	North	South
Dishwashers	98%	105%	97%	103%
Washer-Dryers	102%	100%	100%	101%
Sound Systems	80%	98%	97%	96%
VCRs and Camcorders	101%	102%	103%	104%
Refrigerators	99%	101%	102%	103%

Exhibit 4–6 Evaluation of Product Market Combinations

	Jones' and Woo's Performance in the West	
	Jones	Woo
Dishwashers	103%	104%
Washer-Dryers	110%	111%
Sound Systems	35%	85%
VCRs and Camcorders	110%	110%
Refrigerators	100%	100%

Exhibit 4–7 Comparison of Jones's and Woo's Performance

not do well, it hurt Jones much more readily than Woo. Thus, internal data indicate that Jones should not be fired. Rather, the product needs to be evaluated and, furthermore, product quotas and salespeople's territories need to be examined more carefully. The next area that needs to be considered is advertising.

ADVERTISING CONSIDERATIONS

Internal data can guide advertising activity in a number of ways. Two of these are described in recent experiences at Sears. As the merchandise group's chief executive put Sears back in the black, he closed down 113 poorly performing stores and launched a series of jazzy ads to improve the existing image (*Business Week*, August 15, 1994). Similarly, those merchandise lines and stores that were doing well were given an extra advertising boost for better results.

The third area of advertising that can be facilitated by using internal data is the allocation of advertising dollars among different media. This task is quite difficult but can be approximated by running multiple regressions where the dependent variable is total sales and the independent variables are different media input in dollars. There are many other advertising effectiveness tests discussed later on in this book. However, internal data analysis of this type can reveal good information by which advertising allocations can be reconsidered.

Finally, different types of data sets can be used to evaluate distribution.

EVALUATION OF DISTRIBUTION

Many aspects of distribution can be explored by using internal data. Two of these are discussed here: first, the outlet mix a firm uses, and second, transportation costs.

	Small	Medium	Large
Urban	70	100	150
Rural	120	85	70

Exhibit 4–8 Distribution Effectiveness Index

Assume that a company deals with many retail outlets. With all these considered, the average store sales for the company's products is 100. Exhibit 4–8 illustrates this situation. The company is analyzing its sales using a pattern with which it has classified its retail outlets. As can be seen, in an urban setting, the large retail firms do more than 50 percent of the average in terms of selling the company's products. On the other hand, in rural settings, small firms do more than 20 percent of the average store sale. Thus, if a company were to concentrate large retail stores in urban areas and small retail stores in rural areas as outlets, it would be likely to optimize its distribution outlet mix.

In terms of transportation costs, the firm having established the retail outlet mix can easily explore which stores are subject to either higher or lower transportation costs and where they are located. At this point, it is quite possible for the firm to explore other transportation options. Here, additional data are needed to provide better information for the firm. A final area of exploration is customer satisfaction.

One additional consideration must be touched on: using the sales force as a field intelligence tool (Falvey 1992). Sales managers have exclusive access to the field sales force. If these managers are effective communicators, they can receive much data and information from the field through the sales force. Assuming open communication channels, the field sales force is in an excellent position to assess the firm's position in the market, the degree of product acceptance, typical customer reactions, and the like. Falvey (1992) maintained that sometimes, such information from the field representatives can be less costly and more effective than the data generated by specific market research inputs.

An example of such input from the field sales force comes from the food industry (Grove, LaForge, Knowles, & Stone 1992). All call reports of the field workers, filed over a three-month period, are assembled. Independent judges analyze and classify the contents of the call reports. A matrix is developed so that specific data can be tallied across each salesperson for the whole sales force. The matrix generates specific information from all the data inputs, which information is used to evaluate the overall effectiveness of the sales force.

CUSTOMER SATISFACTION ASSESSMENT

Only one component of customer satisfaction can be assessed by using the internal data of the firm. It is possible to determine whether the regular customers of a company, such as a bank or retail establishment, are leaving or staying with the company. Here, additional information is necessary to find out why the regular customers are behaving as they are. This is perhaps one of the most neglected areas in customer relations. Considering the fact that acquiring new customers is five times more costly than keeping the regular customers happy (Peters 1989), it is extremely astute for the marketing executive to explore this area. Particularly, by using internal data, the marketing decision maker can decide whom to focus on in exit analyses. It is not possible to interview all the customers who left the company; hence, it is important to single out who should be interviewed so that meaningful exit analyses can be performed. All these analyses lead to examining market share and profitability of the firm.

MARKET SHARE AND PROFITABILITY

As the resources of the firm are allocated and reallocated on the basis of internal factual information, the firm's market share and profitability will vary. Profitability in absolute terms can be measured internally. However, it is important to compare the firm's performance to that of its competitors and to industry averages. This can be accomplished in many different ways. There may not be one best way of determining the profitability level of the firm, but it is important for the marketing decision maker to realize the necessity of doing so. Second, the calculation is based on information that must be generated. Third, experience is critical in such attempts to evaluate the firm's profitability.

The firm's market share requires additional outside information in addition to internal data–generated information. Once again, the experienced decision maker can work closely with the information worker to establish certain criteria to be utilized in determining the total market potential or total actual market volume.

OPPORTUNITY INDICATORS

Once internal data have been analyzed to understand the marketing performance of the firm, it is necessary to determine the existing and new market opportunities. This may call for a "SWOT" (Strengths, Weaknesses, Opportunities, Threats) analysis. It must be reiterated that the marketing decision maker here has to work very closely with the firm's information workers. As Exhibit 4–1 indicates, opportunities need to be evaluated so that a carefully designed overall resource allocation can be planned. This resource allocation would indicate just how much to put into areas such as advertising, sales, transportation, product development, and price adjustment. All these are extremely critical tools at the disposal of the marketing decision maker, who must try to put together the most appropriate marketing mix.

SUMMARY

This chapter emphasizes the importance of internal data and explains how it should be used to best advantage. Although accounting typically has access to a gold mine of data, it is up to the marketing decision maker to mine the information. The worst-case scenario is the use of this data gold mine to control marketing activities of the firm without totally understanding what marketing can accomplish in the marketplace.

Internal data can be used to evaluate marketing performance in general and the performance of particular elements of the marketing mix individually. An internal evaluation of the elements of the marketing mix can easily lead to the development of a better mix.

One of the most critical outcomes of internal data analysis is that it indicates when and what kind of additional data are needed so that the marketing decision maker can make better decisions. It is pointed out in this chapter that customer relations, consumer reaction, and developments in the marketplace are all important additional data that can be used to generate the necessary information to make better marketing decisions.

REFERENCES

Falvey, Jack. 1992. "Field Intelligence." *Sales and Marketing Management*, November, 10–12.

Fane, Gary. 1992. "Into the Future: The Controller as Marketer." *Corporate Controller*, January/February, 25-30.

Grove, Stephen J., Mary C. LaForge, Patricia A. Knowles, and Louis H. Stone. 1992. "Improving Sales Call Reporting for Better Management Decisions." *Journal of Consumer Marketing* (Fall): 65–72.

Kotler, Philip. 1994. *Marketing Management*. Englewood Cliffs, NJ: Prentice Hall.

Peters, Tom. 1989. *Thriving on Chaos*. New York: Alfred A. Knopf.

"Sears' Turnaround Is for Real—For Now." *Business Week*, August 15, 1994. 102-3.

Factual Data Collection in Marketing: Observations

INTRODUCTION

One of the simplest and most effective methods of generating marketing information is through firsthand observation. By stationing an observer in a supermarket, for instance, research can generate information as to how shoppers are reacting to a company's newly introduced product or to some of its specific features. Observational techniques can amass a wealth of data and can produce important information for the firm's marketing activities.

Unfortunately, researchers have tended to ignore the advantages of observation as a method of information generation. As early as 1953, Madge pointed out, "first hand preliminary observations are often dispensed with on grounds of lack of time, or through the mistaken belief that all the main features of the points at issue are already known" (117). Thus, marketing researchers have failed to use this highly effective research tool, which is already at their disposal. Almost three decades later, the status of observation research has changed little. Indeed, a cursory look at the existing marketing research books indicates how little emphasis is put on this technique. However, the marketing decision maker should realize that this is a fast, low-cost technique that can generate the type of data that other techniques cannot.

OBSERVATION: A MISUNDERSTOOD TECHNIQUE

The critical mass of marketing research is based upon interviews and questionnaires. Although these tools have their place and, if used properly, can generate significant databases and invaluable information, they are limited to use with accessible people who will cooperate in the survey process. Furthermore, interviews and questionnaires are generally used alone as research techniques. In addition to being practical, quick, and low-cost, observations can generate supplemental information which, to a certain extent, balances out some of the problems of the survey technique. However, observation is a misunderstood technique that is scarcely utilized in marketing research and, hence, is only nominally useful to marketing decision makers (Samli 1967).

Observation has not been used as widely as it should be, nor has it been developed in the more scientific tradition of survey techniques and refined skills in measurement. Since the early 1950s, when marketing and, hence, marketing research came of age, there has been a tradition of developing survey techniques to measure a wide variety of phenomena. Observation, however, has not enjoyed a similar tradition of development and advancement. Perhaps because it is, in some ways, rather simplistic and is not quite scientific-sounding. It is necessary to put observation into the arsenal of marketing researchers as a viable and important research technique.

It must be reiterated that intelligence and expertise are built out of interaction with the environment, not in isolation from it (Sorohan 1993). This is the essence of cognitive research, and observation is a critical part thereof. The decision maker must realize that good data at a low cost can be generated through observation. The critical difference between observation and other research techniques is that with observation there is no need to ask people to recall some action or event, nor any need to rely on individuals' own self-reports.

CHARACTERISTICS OF OBSERVATIONS

In order to systematize and make observation techniques more scientific, a five-step activity can be utilized (Exhibit 5–1). There may be slightly different versions of this five-step procedure. However, the general orientation presented here is quite appropriate for any kind of observational research (Grove & Fisk 1992; Wedberg 1990; Seymour 1988).

Step one revolves around the concept to be researched. All phenomena have certain critical aspects, the understanding of which will provide complete comprehension for the specific phenomenon. For instance, an evaluation of the performance of a department in a department store may be achieved by determining if the people like the

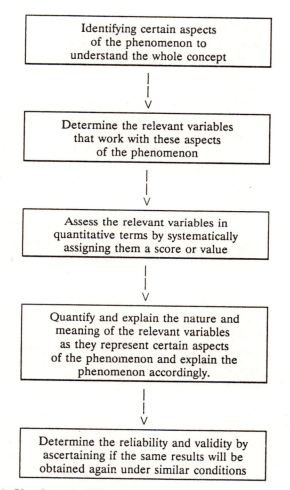

Exhibit 5–1 Key Steps in Observation Research

displays and the merchandise, find the department attractive, and so forth. Understanding the performance of the department is critical, and certainly determining that it is an attractive and popular department is quite critical for management.

Observation research assumes, for instance, that consumer behavior patterns are caused by a number of antecedent conditions, circumstances, or events. Thus, the conditions, circumstances, or events that may have causal relationships to the phenomenon in question need to be carefully identified.

Step two involves determining the relevant variables that work with the antecedent conditions, circumstances, or events that would explain the phenomenon or certain parts of it, and for which more information is required.

Since there are many, the researcher must carefully analyze variable factors, determine which ones are particularly relevant, and make proper allowances to approximate them. Approximating the variables will explain the phenomenon.

Continuing on with the department store example, assume that this is a children's wear department and further assume that "back-to-school" displays are being presented. The effectiveness of this department in this case may be related to how well it is doing at this critical juncture, the back-to-school period. The criteria to determine the effectiveness of this promotion are multiple. Just how many people notice it? What are their facial expressions? How many people walked in and touched the merchandise? How many people inquired about the merchandise? The marketing decision maker, who is not going to make a decision as to how the observation process should take place but is going to use the results of the process, must realize that the outcome of this research activity will show how this department is doing long before the sales and financial results are analyzed and the profit and loss statements are prepared. Thus, if properly developed, this kind of information provides a much-needed advance indication of the department's performance. This early indicator facilitates early evaluation and adjustment. By the time the financial results have been developed and analyzed, it is too late for early adjustment and improved performance.

The third step is the assessment of the variables for observation. The researcher must carefully identify the relevant variables and determine how certain values or scores can be assigned to them. Unless the variables are quantified, they cannot be analyzed, compared, and contrasted. They need to be reduced to a common denominator, typically numbers. At this point, the research findings are expressed in quantifiab terms. Unless qualitative data are quantified, meaningful statistical analyses cannot be performed. Such analyses facilitate understanding and in-depth analysis of research efforts and will guide the decision maker.

Step four is basically quantification and actual research activity. Quantification can be a simple counting of easily observable variables, such as increased traffic to the department, or it can be much more complicated and subjective, such as assessing the facial expressions as to the people's approval or disapproval of a display. The observer subjectively has to determine the shopper's reaction and quantify it. Thus, the result would be the data indicating how many shoppers

Department Average Traffic	New Promotion Traffic	Interest Score	Purchase Number of Transactions
100%	140%	120%	120%

Exhibit 5–2 Observation Research Results

reacted negatively and how many reacted positively and, perhaps, how many reacted very positively. The observation of positive versus negative reactions may be further associated with purchases.

Exhibit 5–2 illustrates this situation. Assuming that the typical departmental traffic is 100 percent, the new promotional display obviously attracted a lot of attention, since on the same index base the traffic went up to 140 percent. Although it attracted a lot of attention, not all people liked it. The interest score, which is developed subjectively by observing people's reactions, went up only by 20 index points, indicating that some people did not like the new display.

One additional bit of data is obtained from Exhibit 5–2. If purchases are to be compared with attention-getting versus interest-generating features of the display, it becomes clear that sales are more closely related to the display's interest-generating features. This may lead to a critical decision such as attempting to generate more interest on the part of the prospective purchasers by designing the display accordingly.

The observational study indicated how many shoppers who reacted negatively still purchased in the department being observed. Similarly, the research pointed out that a certain percentage of those who reacted positively purchased in the department. Thus, through observation, it is possible to determine whether a positive reaction to, say, a special display, caused an increase in sales. Of course, at this point observation research data may be supplemented with survey data and the customers may, selectively, be questioned on subjects such as the specific features of the display that attracted them.

Step five involves establishing validity and reliability of the gathered data. The validity of the observation research data needs to be established before the research findings are used in the firm's decision-making process. Do the data indicate what they mean to? Even though observation research may indicate poor shopper reaction to a particular display, the display may not be entirely at fault. The display's location may be poor, it may include too few shelf facings or contain inadequate stock levels. Similarly, the wrong people may have been observed, or observation may have taken place at the wrong hours.

Other factors may have distorted the research findings. For example, competitors may have recently increased their advertising. Thus, it is important that prevailing conditions as well as specific observed events be noted for an effective diagnosis of causal relationships. It is particularly important that observation research findings be assessed in light of outside factors that may have affected the outcome.

To measure reliability, it is necessary to determine the extent to which a given phenomenon can be accurately observed, measured, or inferred. It is desirable to determine that the observation data are reliable and that under similar circumstances, a similar effort will yield the same type of results. Consistent results suggest a high reliability factor, while inconsistent results suggest the opposite.

The consistency of results should be considered in making marketing decisions. If the number of shelf facings is proportional to the sales level in various different instances or departments, then the marketing decision maker can safely assume that concentrating on installing more shelf facings is the proper way of proceeding. However, if the observation research results have shown, for instance, that both high and low level of sales have taken place with the same level of shelf facings, the marketing decision maker will be well advised to investigate further before deciding to put large resources into additional shelf facings.

THE DECISION MAKER'S POSITION

The marketing decision maker who is likely to use these data must ask a number of key questions. These are listed in Exhibit 5–3.

Perhaps the most important question is whether the results of observation research should lead to a critical marketing decision. The case that has been used for illustration thus far indicates that if the promotion can create a certain amount of interest, it is useful. The same logic could be applied to all the departments of a department store. In this case, it may be necessary to develop the displays or the concepts and use focus groups (small groups composed of typical customers) to react. Here, there may be a need for additional information. However, as far as the children's department is concerned, the display was a success and would continue until the back-to-school rush is over.

The second question the decision maker needs to ask is whether the study was conducted properly? This would include considering how the data were gathered, how good were the reliability and validity features, and whether critical decisions could be based on this level of data quality.

The third question relates to whether additional data are needed. The marketing decision maker must be in a position not only to evaluate the results of the observation study conducted but also to determine whether these results are sufficient to make a decision. It is possible, for

Do observation study results indicate a clear-cut decision situation?

Was the study conducted properly?

Are additional data needed?

Can these data be acquired by additional observation study?

Should there be supplemental data by using another data gathering technique?

How factual are the data?

Exhibit 5–3 Marketing Decision Makers' Questions

instance, that the observation study objectively counted the new promotion traffic (Exhibit 5–2) but did not attempt to develop interest scores, which would have required more subjective input. As seen in Exhibit 5–2, interest scores are more critical for sales estimates. If the marketing decision maker is not familiar with the research technique and the resultant database, he or she will not have the wisdom to ask for additional research data in order to make better decisions.

The illustration above indicates that additional observation would have been necessary. This is the fourth question. If more data are needed, can these be acquired by observational techniques? The decision maker not only should be in a position to decide if additional information is necessary, but should also be capable of specifying how this additional information may be obtained. This brings us to the next to last question in Exhibit 5–3.

Should there be supplemental data gathered by using other research techniques? It is possible that the results of the observation technique alone may not be sufficient. Therefore, the marketing decision maker is in an enviable position and can specify what these additional data needs are and how they may be obtained. It is, again, extremely critical that the marketing decision maker be in a position to guide the research team in the right direction.

Finally, how factual are the data? Stafford (1993) pointed out that participant observation is particularly well suited for gaining an insider's perspective about the surroundings and behavior. However, participant observation may create the opportunity for more subjective evaluation of the conditions of the observation. Here, *simple tallying* may give way to *subjective evaluation*, such as whether the participant thinks the salesperson is doing a *good job*. At this point, the results of these efforts cease to be factual. The marketing decision maker must be informed about the observational methodology. The results of simple tallying and observations through mechanical devices such as registering the number of people entering the drug store are strictly factual. However, subjective observations must be closely scrutinized either by the researcher or by the decision maker.

SUMMARY

This chapter presents a knowledge base for the least understood and most widely neglected data gathering technique: observation.

Observations are particularly good activities because they are quick, economical, practical, and relatively easy, to carry out. Much data can easily be amassed by using this research technique.

A five-step research process is used on observations. It must be dcided (1) what needs to be studied, (2) how observations can explain the phenomenon, and (3) how the observation should be conducted; then it is necessary to (4) develop the measurement base and quantify and analyze the results, and (5) determine the validity and reliability features of the study.

Once the results of the observation study have been received, the marketing decision maker must answer at least five key questions: (1) Is this enough for a clear-cut decision? (2) Are the data of good quality? (3) Do I need additional data? (4) Is there a need for additional observation data? (5) Should there be supplemental data generated by other research techniques?

REFERENCES

Grove, Stephen J., and Raymond P. Fisk. 1992. "Observational Data Collection Method for Services Marketing: An Overview." *Journal of the Academy of Marketing Science* (Summer): 217–24.

Madge, John. 1953. *The Tools of Social Science*. London: Longmans, Green and Co.

Samli, A. Coskun. 1967. "Observations as a Means of Fact Gathering for Marketing Decisions." *Business Perspectives*, Fall, 19–24.

Seymour, Daniel T. 1988. *Marketing Research*. Chicago, IL: Probus.

Sorohan, Erica Gordon. 1993. "We Do Therefore We Learn." *Training and Development*, October, 47–55.

Stafford, Marla Royne. 1993. "Participant Observation and the Pursuit of Truth: Methodological and Ethical Considerations." *Journal of the Marketing Research Society* (January): 63–76.

Wedberg, George H. 1990. "But First, Understand the Problem." *Journal of Systems Management* (June): 20–28.

Generating Data Through Surveys

INTRODUCTION

Survey research is the key data collection technique to rely on direct questioning. Most of the data used in marketing research are generated by survey research techniques. All three types of data—facts, attitudes, and motives—are generated in this way. However, the instruments used in gathering these three types are quite different. This chapter presents a discussion of survey techniques and what marketing decision makers should know about data generated through surveys. It must be realized that marketing as a process needs information regarding the market and how the firm should interact with it. The data about the market are typically generated through surveys.

TYPES OF SURVEYS

There are three basic survey research techniques: (1) the telephone survey, (2) the mail survey, and (3) the personal interview. Each of these has unique advantages and disadvantages. The selection process of the most appropriate technique is dependent upon the judgment of the marketing decision maker concerning the specific information needs.

Exhibit 6–1 illustrates the key characteristics of the three survey techniques. They are examined on the basis of three different groups: (1) features, (2) special advantages, and (3) special disadvantages.

Features	Technique		
	Mail	Telephone	Personal Interview
Response Generating Ability	Low	High	Very High
Respondent Convenience	Very High	Very Low	Low
Information Obtaining Ability	High	Low	Very High
Practicality to Manage	High	Very High	Low
Ease of Processing	Very High	High	Low*
Possibility of Response Bias	Very High	High	Low
Special Advantages			
Sequential Control of Information	Low	High	Very High
Special Incentive to Participate	Low	High	Very High
Ability to Generate In-Depth Information	High	Low	Very High
Special Disadvantages			
Proportion of No-response	Very High	Low	Very Low
Need for Special Expertise to Administer	Low	High	Very High
Need for Special Expertise to Analyze	Low	High	Very High
Cost Factor	Low	Low	High
Quality of Data	High	Low	Very High

*It is assumed that in personal interviews there is always a greater opportunity to use unstructured and indirect questions.

Exhibit 6–1 Key Features of the Three Survey Techniques

Features

Mail surveys do not generate much response. However, on the other end of the spectrum, personal interviews can stimulate high levels of response. Telephone surveys are typically also quite effective in generating response.

Mail surveys are very good in regard to the respondent's convenience. He or she can respond to the survey by filling out the questionnaire at any time. Telephone surveys present the worst problem in terms of the respondent's convenience because they need to be answered right then and there. They need to be conducted within a certain time frame so that the respondents will be contacted at home. This condition sets serious constraints as to when the survey can be conducted, and may compel it to take place during certain inconvenient times.

Of the three survey techniques, the personal interview is most likely to entice the respondents to participate in the study, and trained interviewers are capable of generating the necessary data.

Of the three techniques, the simplest to manage is the telephone survey. It is, by definition, simpler because it is more brief and straightforward. Quite seldom is there a telephone survey that will generate attitudinal and motivational data. On the other hand, personal interviews are quite difficult to manage. Surveys that revolve around indepth interviews are particularly difficult to conduct, quantify, and interpret.

Ease of processing is closely related to the practicality of management. Mail surveys typically are designed in advance for specific processing. Quite often, the coding system and analysis to be performed are designed together with the questionnaire, in advance. Thus, processing is better planned and controlled in mail surveys. In telephone surveys, processing is rather simpler since the nature of the survey is also short and simple. Personal interviews are substantially more difficult in terms of generating coding and processing the data.

Response bias is always a very critical factor to consider in surveys. In mail surveys, the respondents have much time to think and perhaps rationalize their answers, rather than be factual. Furthermore, they know where the questionnaire is leading, which makes it more tempting to adjust the answers according to the overall direction of the computer. In personal interviews, this problem does not exist as the interviewers are trained to detect and eliminate response bias.

Special Advantages

The sequential control of information, if done improperly, will lead to response bias. It may be quite important for the respondents not to know what the next question is in order to avoid unintentionally biasing their responses. Personal interviews naturally are best for this situation. Telephone surveys are also good, but mail surveys may be quite problematic.

Personal interviews also provide a special incentive for prospects to participate in the survey. Interviewers are trained to lure the prospective respondents to participate. There is a certain type of attraction in survey participation. Mail surveys, however, yield a very low level of participation. Anytime a survey receives about a 15 percent response, it is considered to be quite good. Telephone surveys are somewhat better than mail surveys, perhaps because they are rather brief and somewhat interesting (with a real person on the other end of the telephone line).

Finally, by definition, personal interviews generate much more indepth data and subsequent information than any other survey technique. This is due to the fact that the interviewer is trained and the study is designed in such a way to produce much additional in-depth information. Mail surveys also provide some in-depth information because they are longer than telephone surveys and, therefore, they can reach out and generate more data. However, they cannot be as good in this area as personal interviews.

Special Disadvantages

It is critical for a marketing decision maker to understand that the quality of data and cost are two alternatives. There is always a trade-off between the two. It is up to the decision maker to decide what quality of data is needed for the decision on hand that will also be cost-effective, which means that an acceptable sum is allotted for this project that is within the constraints of the budget and in line with other research activities. In other words, the analysis will not take unnecessary sums of money away from other projects. Exhibit 6–1 points out some of the special disadvantages of the three survey techniques.

Nonresponse

In mail surveys, there is an extremely high percentage of non-response. Unfortunately, somewhere around 10 to 14 percent is considered to be a reasonable response rate for mail surveys. This is obviously very low, and it creates strong pressure to verify the survey results because if the response does not represent, say, the firm's target market, then the survey results can be extremely misleading. On the other end of the spectrum, personal interviews are usually well responded to by American consumers. This is particularly true in typical college towns, where research is a constant, ongoing activity. Americans appear to glorify somebody's interest in their opinions and reasoning. In their minds there may be some connection between their being interviewed and celebrities being interviewed by the members of the press.

Special Expertise

Both telephone surveys and personal interviews call for interpersonal communication skills. In personal interviews, these skills are extremely critical. The ability to put the respondent at ease and encourage participation calls for proper training. Additionally, the interviewer keeps the respondent's interest up and reports the results of the interview accurately. If the study is more in-depth and is related to, say, motivation or attitudes, the interviewer may have to be specially trained. It is clear that the role of the interviewer is very critical for the survey, and therefore, proper training is a necessary ingredient. In mail surveys there are no special skills required, because there is no interview. Needless to say, in all three cases—mail, telephone, and personal interview—questionnaire design is extremely important so that the necessary data can be gathered. For this function, the needed skills are the same in all three types of questionnaires.

Analysis

Just as in administering surveys, in analyzing survey data, special expertise is needed. Particularly in motivational and attitudinal studies, interpretation becomes extremely critical. Much of the time, analyzing and interpreting personal interviews requires some psychological expertise. This situation makes personal interviews more demanding and difficult to use.

Cost Factor

Because of the special needs of personnel, expertise, and time, personal interviews cost much more than other forms of surveys. However, personal interviews are the only instruments that generate in-depth data on attitudes and motives. Hence, they are very important for generating special data.

Quality

Finally, the quality of the data is related to the fact that personal interviews are planned and calculated. If they are properly executed, they provide more valuable data than other techniques. Because they produce limited and superficial data, telephone interviews are considered to generate only a low quality of data. Mail surveys also, because of their limited returns, provide less than adequate data for many uses. Thus, the marketing decision maker must be aware of the quality and cost trade-off alternatives and know which survey technique can yield better results for the problem that is being considered.

In understanding data generated by surveys, the marketing decision maker must have a good idea as to how the data are generated and what kinds of questions will yield what kind of data.

TYPES OF QUESTIONS

Regardless of what type of survey technique is utilized, there are different types of questions that yield different types of data. Without a knowledge of these types of questions and the nature of the data they generate, it will be impossible to yield effective survey results.

	Direct	Indirect
Structure Structured	Dichotomous Multiple choice Checklists, etc. (mostly facts)	Different types of scales (opinion and attitude research)
Unstructured	Open-ended questions (mostly facts and opinions)	Various types of projective techniques (motivation research)

Exhibit 6–2 Types of Questions and the Nature of the Data They Generate

Exhibit 6–2 portrays the two basic dimensions of questioning, within which a number of known types of questions are listed. This table is by no means all-inclusive but can be effective in alerting the reader to the specific patterns in questioning.

The two dimensions are *structure* and *directness*. These two dimensions represent two separate spectra, and the choice, therefore, extends beyond a simple two-by-two matrix. However, the two-by-two matrix basically reflects the clear-cut categories.

The horizontal dimension in Exhibit 6–2 deals with how the question was asked. This dimension refers to the degree of disguise in the manner of questioning. There are many situations where the specific bits of data sought cannot be obtained directly from the respondent. For instance, a question such as, "Do you think medicine must taste bad to be good?" is a leading question and will yield biased data. In such cases, the question may be asked indirectly by using two separate questions. The questions may be:

Is your medicine powerful?

☐ powerful   ☐ not so powerful

How does your medicine taste?

☐ good   ☐ bad

A similar situation may be related to a mouthwash.

Does your mouthwash feel stronger than other mouthwashes you have tried?

☐ stronger   ☐ weaker

Do you think your mouthwash lasts longer than other mouthwashes
you have tried?

☐ lasts longer   ☐ does not last longer

The second dimension is structure. Structure is related to the format
of the question. If the question is highly structured, it has a set format.
The choice of answers is specified, and instructions are clear as to how
to answer the question. The question may have just a simple yes or no
answer or a clearly spelled-out checklist. On the other hand, if a question is unstructured, it asks the respondent to fill in the blank space and
answer freely.

Within these two dimensions, there are at least four key groups of
questioning styles. As seen in Exhibit 6–2, each group is located in one
cell.

Direct-Structured

These are direct and simplistic questions, which yield primarily facts.
They are easiest to answer and are used most often in telephone surveys.

Structured-Indirect

As illustrated earlier, if trying to test a hypothesis would create a
biased answer, then it may be asked indirectly. A hypothesis is a proposed explanation for a problem or a situation, the testing of which will
be very important for the decision process of the firm. Most attitudinal
studies and opinion polls are likely to have indirect questioning practices, which are best in generating attitudinal data.

Unstructured-Direct

In many cases, it is not possible to have an accurate list of possible
answers, nor is it possible to predict the response. In such situations, it
is critical to get the respondent to answer the question freely and
directly. Open-ended questions are designed for this purpose. They
yield factual data as well as data related to opinions.

Unstructured-Indirect

This is probably the most difficult approach to generating meaningful
marketing data. Here the data cannot be obtained directly but also must
be generated in an unstructured fashion. This is the only way in which

marketing can generate motivation-related data. As will be discussed in chapters 11 and 12, this type of data and subsequent information is very critical for many marketing decisions.

COMMUNICATING WITH RESPONDENTS IN SURVEYS

Although the marketing decision maker is not involved in the preparation of the survey instrument, there are a number of features needed in these instruments to generate the necessary data objectively and adequately. This whole process of questionnaire development is based on the following principles:

1. The questionnaire must be worded in the simplest and most straightforward manner.
2. The questions should not lead the respondent to feel pressured to answer them in a certain, biased way.
3. The questions must be directed toward the respondents' areas of competency. If the respondents do not know a subject, they cannot answer.
4. The questionnaire must generate the desired database rather than redundant data.
5. The questionnaire format must be most suited for coding, processing, and analysis.
6. Every question must have a reason to be in the questionnaire and must have a place in the questionnaire.
7. If respondents experience difficulty in answering certain questions, these must be readily identifiable.
8. The length of the questionnaire may not be critical as long as the respondents' interest can be maintained. However, the length issue should not be dismissed lightly.
9. There should be a logical order for the questions in the questionnaire, which should enhance the respondents' willingness to participate.
10. The questionnaire should satisfy the relevancy, validity, and reliability requirements of any good survey research project.

CONCERNS OF THE MARKETING DECISION MAKER

General Foods has developed guidelines to generate and maintain quality data for the company (Hambaugh 1989). Although it is the responsibility of the researcher, the marketing decision maker has to ensure that the information generated from the data is of high quality and deals specifically with the decision area in question. General Foods' approach involves three steps. First, clearly stated expectations for survey work are developed and made available for all research workers, as well as decision makers. Second, feedback methods are established on completed survey work. This feedback may help improve the survey procedures used in data gathering. Third, a method of validation must be established. Among others, this point will automatically go to respondents and confirm some of their responses. Once the marketing decision maker has been assured of the quality and value of the data, it is easier for the data-driven information to be used for critical marketing decisions.

It is assumed that the questionnaire construction activity is the key responsibility of the research workers. This responsibility should not be taken lightly. If the survey instrument is inadequate, it will be impossible to generate valuable data. The marketing decision maker who is very familiar with the information needs may provide some guidance to research workers in the construction of survey instruments.

In Exhibit 2–2, the research process was presented and the responsibilities of different parties were identified. Identifying the research problem, establishing research objectives, formulating information needs, determining specific types of information, pinpointing information sources, deciding on the research technique to be used, developing the instruments for data gathering, and, finally, gather the data and converting them into information are all the researchers' responsibility. However, some scholars think that the decision maker must be involved in these stages or at least must have good knowledge of activities preceding the generation of information before it is used for decisions (Worchester & Downham 1986; Goyder 1966).

It is maintained here that the decision-maker must have a reasonable understanding of how the data will look once they are converted into information. Otherwise, the whole process may become very costly and time-consuming. However, it is also maintained here that the decision maker must not spend too much time and effort in the information generation aspect of the total activity.

THE SOURCE OF INFORMATION

The marketing decision maker certainly does not need to be an expert in sampling. (This is an important topic on which much has been written.) However, the decision maker must be familiar with certain issues that are critical to the decision-making process.

Typically, marketing data are generated through marketing research. This research extracts the data from a sample. A number of things must be known about samples:

1. What is the definition of the universe from which the sample was taken? Naturally, a set of data on the elderly cannot be obtained from a sample of young adults.
2. The decision maker must also know if the variables that are explored in this sample are the critical ones that will generate the information that the firm needs.
3. How is the sample designed? What are the units used in the sample (housing units, individual teenagers, children, etc.)
4. How are the sample units selected? The procedure that is used here is very critical for statisticians and the researchers. There are two major sampling techniques: (1) probability sampling, and (2) nonprobability sampling.

In probability samples, all the elements of the universe have an equal opportunity to be included in the sample. The decision maker must realize that this kind of sample may provide a better database; however, it will also be substantially more costly. Probability (or random) samples provide greater opportunity for the use of a large variety of statistical techniques. These are *parametric* statistical techniques. All of them can be based on the basic premise of sample randomness.

However, for marketing, quite often nonprobability samples can generate better databases. This is because they may have a purpose, such as interviewing customers who shop at a store primarily during weekends. In such cases, a "purposive" sample is better for generating the necessary database. In nonrandom (or nonprobability) samples, there are numerous nonparametric techniques that are quite versatile and adequate for data analyses and information generation, although parametric statistical techniques cannot be used for data analyses.

There are also a few hybrid sampling techniques that combine both probability and nonprobability characteristics. Three such techniques are briefly discussed here: stratified random samples, cluster samples, and area samples.

Stratified random samples are based on the assumption that the universe can be broken down into numerous strata. The units within a stratum are standardized. In other words, they are very similar. The greater the similarity among the stratum units and the greater the differences among the strata, the more effective is this sampling technique. On a random basis, units from each stratum are chosen for the sample.

Cluster sampling is the opposite of stratified random sampling. The universe here is also broken into clusters. Here, however, each and every cluster represents the universe in its own right. The greater the heterogeneity among the cluster units within the cluster and the greater the similarity among the clusters, the more effective the cluster sampling technique. Here, a few of the clusters are chosen on a random basis to develop the sample.

Finally, area sampling is related to universes that have a geographic dimension. A city, a town, or a state can be a universe. Here, some neighborhoods may be diversified enough to represent the whole city. In such a case, some version of cluster sampling may be utilized. Similarly, throughout the city there may be very homogeneous neighborhoods. In such a case, a variation of stratified random sample may be used to develop the sample.

It must be reiterated that if the sample is not appropriate, the database generated through the survey or observation is not likely to provide a good information base. Thus, good marketing decisions must start with good samples, which are not necessarily random but are appropriate in terms of generating the relevant data.

SUMMARY

This chapter deals with survey data as they are needed by marketing decision makers. Different survey techniques are discussed, and their strengths and weaknesses are presented. Three survey techniques—mail, telephone, and personal interviews—are analyzed. Their analyses are concentrated on their specific features and their special advantages and disadvantages. Types of questions are also explored in this chapter. Questioning styles are explored from the perspective of two separate dimensions, directness and structure.

Finally, a special attempt is made to make sure that marketing decision-makers are assured of the quality and value of the survey data–driven information to be a valuable support for critical marketing decisions.

REFERENCES

Davies, Richard. 1986. "Omnibus Surveys." In *Consumer Market Research Handbook*, ed. Robert T. Worchester and John Downham, 231–44. Amsterdam: ESOMAR, North Holland.

Goyder, John. 1966. "Surveys on Surveys: Limitations and Potentialities." *Public Opinion Quarterly* 50:27–41.

Hambaugh, Pam. 1989. "Survey Research Quality: The Extra Value of the Extra Step." *Journal of Advertising Research* (January–July): 3–9.

Worchester, Robert M., and John Downham (eds.). 1986. *Consumer Market Research Handbook*, Amsterdam: ESOMAR, North Holland.

Data Generation
Through Experiments

INTRODUCTION

Experiments in marketing, as in the biological sciences, are carefully planned in advance and are designed to generate new and very specific knowledge. This knowledge is primarily in the area of causation. As in other social sciences, ascertaining causative relationships in marketing is difficult and subject to frequent error. This is due to the impossibility of controlling extraneous variables in an experiment, thus making it virtually impossible to duplicate previous conditions in repeating an experiment in order to confirm previous results.

There are certain types of information that can be generated by experimentation or by pseudo-experiments with which the marketing decision maker should be familiar, as an experiment, for instance, on the expected increase in the sales volume based on the decline in price or the change in the sales volume due to a new advertising campaign is extremely critical. The results of these experiments may lead to either keeping the price as is and advertising differently or keeping advertising as is and reducing the price. Once again, there is a tradeoff between the quality of data and the cost. The marketing decision maker must be familiar with what the experimental procedures can and cannot accomplish. This chapter deals with, first, the classical experimentation procedures and, then, specific procedures to deviate from classical experiments are discussed. Finally, modern computerized experimental techniques are analyzed.

CLASSICAL EXPERIMENTATION

In classical experimental designs, only two discrete items or situations are considered in seeking to establish a causal relationship. In this type of experimental design, causality is assumed whenever a phenomenon occurs in the presence of a given factor, and conversely, lack of causality is assumed if the phenomenon does not occur in the presence of the same factor.

To establish causality, two separate observations (or two sets of observations) are required: experimental and control situations. In fact, the use of a control situation in conjunction with an experimental situation is the principal basis for distinguishing experimentation from surveys and other less precise methods of data gathering. While a great deal of useful marketing data is accumulated through nonexperimental methods, cause-and-effect relationships cannot be determined because of the lack of control situations. For example, consider the situation in which a newly designed package is introduced for a certain product in one market while the old package is retained in a second. All else remaining the same, an increase in the sales volume in the first market can be attributed to the new packaging design.

DEFINITION AND MECHANICS OF EXPERIMENTATION

Experimentation in marketing implies an attempt to establish causation by having a control mechanism and manipulating a specific phenomenon. There are two approaches to establishing causal relationships through experimentation. First, the regular course of the phenomenon may be altered deliberately by the experimenter. Thus, in order to evaluate the impact of special displays on impulse buying, a special experimental situation may be set up by establishing a special product display in one location while in another location making no change in the conditions under which the same product is offered to the consumer. For example, a special display by Pepsi-Cola, complete with posters and other display materials, may be set up in one part of a supermarket (experimental condition). Meanwhile, Pepsi-Cola is also being sold in its regular setting next to other soft drinks in another section of the store (control). The change in the Pepsi sales, thus, can be traced to the special display by keeping track of sales volumes in each of the two locations.

Exhibit 7–1 illustrates this classical experimental model. If the results (sales, in this case) of the experimental situation (Δ) is greater than the control situation (Δ^1), a causality is established between special displays and sales. By the same token, if $\Delta < \Delta^1$, then it is established that

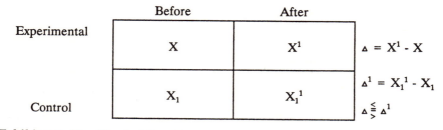

Exhibit 7–1 The Classical Experimental Model

special displays are not effective in stimulating the sales volume. This is the general orientation in classical experiments. There are many other considerations and nuances in the implications, but the general direction of the experiment will be clear, and knowledge of this type can be extremely important.

The second way of establishing a causal relationship is by permitting the phenomenon to run its full course at least twice. In the first instance, the suspected underlying factors are permitted to remain as is, while in the second instance, some of these factors are removed. Thus, to study sales volume for a particular product at a specific sales outlet, for instance, the sales volumes at the location are examined and an analysis is conducted, testing a different way of marketing the product in the same store (such as eliminating promotion for the product, removing the display, changing the price, etc.) and again keeping track of the changes in the sales volumes. The same results as those displayed in Exhibit 7–1 still apply, except that instead of conducting the experiment in, say, two different places, it is conducted in the same place within two different time periods. Causality can be established in either case.

THE TEST AND CONTROL DICHOTOMY

It is understood from our discussion thus far that in experiments, data gathering can be done in terms of surveys, observations, and other types of data. In experimental situations, there are always experimental and control markets or experimental and control groups.

There are a number of criteria that confront the researcher in the choice of test (experimental) and control markets (or areas). There are at least eight such criteria: (1) similar to each other, (2) similar to target markets, (3) economically diversified, (4) economic autonomy, (5) progressive, (6) proper communication facilities, (7) proper distribution facilities, and (8) interest in the product.

CRITERIA FOR TEST AND CONTROL MARKETS

Test and control markets must be similar to each other if the experiment is to be valid. Otherwise, while a test market is being used for the experiment, the control will be unreliable. The two markets not only must be similar to each other but also must reflect the key features of the firm's target markets. In other words, if the firm's products are geared for youth, the experimental and control areas cannot be composed of older people.

Test and control markets must be economically diversified. Single-industry towns are too greatly influenced by economic changes to be good for experiments. For instance, if the economy of a city is overly dependent on the automotive industry and the automotive industry is doing quite well, then the city may be more inclined to buy a new improved outboard motor, not because of its design or genuine interest in the product, but primarily because people are making good money and are not afraid of trying expensive new products. However, this attitude may be construed as genuine interest in the product, and thus the test results will be distorted.

Economic autonomy is somewhat similar to economic diversification in the sense that if the test market has an economy that is dependent on another neighboring economy, then the response to the study cannot be considered totally reliable. Just as in the case of economic autonomy, here, also, the results will be distorted.

The need for assessing the progressiveness of the community implies that declining towns, such as old mining or agricultural towns, are not right for test marketing. They have too many built-in biases to provide objective data.

The test town needs to have certain types of communication facilities that are consistent with the marketing plans, say, for a new product. For example, if the town does not have its own local TV stations, and the product in question requires heavy TV advertising, then the proposed test market is inadequate.

Distribution facilities also need to be adequate. If the product in question needs to be distributed through a series of department stores but the proposed test town does not have such retailing facilities, that town is not adequate. Finally, a reasonable level of interest in the product is necessary. If the proposed test town is located in the Sun Belt and the product being tested is a new type of snow tire, this is not a good match for test marketing.

These are some of the key criteria in choosing test and control markets. The marketing decision maker, once again, must at least be in a position to evaluate the choice of test and control markets. Because marketing experiments are very costly, there has been a strong tendency to deviate from the classical experimentation model. Thus, pseudo-experiments were developed.

PSEUDO-EXPERIMENTS

Exhibit 7–2 illustrates four different variations of classical experiments with short-cuts. The after-only experiment implies not having

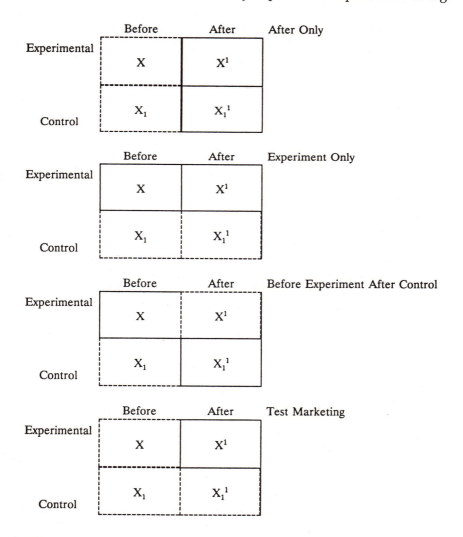

Exhibit 7–2 Various Pseudo-Experiments

past experience or information. This situation can happen if a new product is marketed in, say, the conventional way in the control area and marketed unconventionally in the test area. For instance, assume that Citizen Watches has developed a new product. While in the control area this is marketed in Citizen's conventional way through jewelry stores, in the test area, the company may decide to distribute the new product only through up-scale boutiques and specialty stores.

The experiment-only option indicates that for some reason, the control element is not present. Quite often, this is caused by excessive cost factors. The product, advertising campaign, new package, or whatever is being subjected to this type of experiment, has past data in the experimental area, and as the changes in sales (changes) are incorporated through the results of the "after" situation, the effectiveness of the changes is explained.

The before-experiment, after-control option is based on the impossibility of going back to the experiment group for after data. For instance, a national sample before the Salk vaccine was developed would show X number of polio cases. A similar, but not identical, sample would indicate X_1 number of polio cases. The difference between the two would indicate the effectiveness of the Salk vaccine in eliminating polio.

Finally, the only-after option is related to straight test-marketing, which is particularly important in introducing new products. If a product is introduced nationally and does not do well, the company will lose very large sums of money. A test market can easily reduce this loss. It has been claimed that many companies have reduced the new product failure rate in this way. Particularly in recent years, test marketing has gained popularity. As this popularity has increased, new and better techniques of test marketing have also emerged. Among these new techniques are: (1) using technology, (2) short-term testing, and (3) electronic test marketing.

Using Technology

Particularly in industrial marketing areas, test marketers expose a basic technology to key users and then use their feedback to more precisely target the features and performance of the final product. In recent years, Chrysler and 3M have been searching for ways to shorten the developmental cycle for their new products. Simultaneously, they have improved both the products' quality and their customer acceptance. Both companies built a special facility to encourage researchers and marketers to work in unison rather than sequentially in the development of new products. In fact, it is believed that in the near future, test-marketing will become part of the product development process in industrial marketing. Thus, customers' product-specific needs will be simultaneously handled as the product is developed (Blount 1992).

Other new industrial, institutional, and business-to-business products also are being tested intensively on-site. In most cases the tests are conducted with five to fifty clients and can last anywhere from two to six months (Stern 1991).

Short-Term Testing

Most manufacturers would like to bring new products into the market having been tested and accepted by consumers as quickly as possible. Anheuser-Busch, for instance, took a new beer product, Michelob Dry, from four test markets to national distribution in just two months, after consumer reaction was found to be favorable. In this way, the company managed to move quickly to accumulate market share ahead of its competition (Seeling 1989).

Electronic Test-Marketing

The introduction of new products is costly, and test-marketing activity typically does not yield fast results. This situation increases the launching costs of new products. One of the primary reasons for using electronic test markets is to determine the public's immediate response to new products. For instance, the outdoor barbecue season is limited. In order to accelerate the test market activity, Kraft used an electronic system called Behavior Scan. With this system's quick response mechanism, Kraft tested Bull's-Eye barbecue sauce. The quick response enabled the company to evaluate different levels of advertising, premium pricing, and how well the product was likely to be accepted (Brennan 1988). The computerized response mechanism to questionnaires in a test market situation can accelerate the process and yield more detailed data.

Test-marketing does not have to be strictly consumer-directed. In many cases, middlemen (i.e., retailers and wholesalers) may play a greater role in getting a new product accepted.

TEST-MARKETING WITH CONSUMERS VERSUS MIDDLEMEN

Certain products that have strong brand recognition and brand loyalty can be *pulled* through the distribution system. This pulling process can be achieved by appealing directly to the ultimate consumer. The ultimate consumer, in return, puts pressure on the retailers and whole-

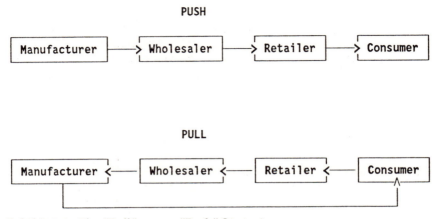

Exhibit 7–3 The "Pull" versus "Push" Strategies

salers to carry this product and distribute it as much as they can (Exhibit 7–3). Some new products, if accepted by the market, will fall in this category. Before launching, these products need to be tested in the market among prospective consumers.

However, there are other products that need to be *pushed* through the market. In many cases, these products are at the mercy of the middlemen. They are accepted in the market only to the extent that middlemen push these products through the distribution system. This situation is depicted by Exhibit 7–3. These products, first and foremost, need to be tested, not in the marketplace among consumers, but among the distributors. In other words, for the products that need to be pushed, trade acceptance is more critical than market (or consumer) acceptance. If the trade likes the product, it can push it to the consumers and, chances are, the product that is being tested and accepted by the trade will be successful in the marketplace.

CONSUMER ACCEPTANCE VERSUS TRADE ACCEPTANCE

Exhibit 7–4 illustrates the contrast between the two types of testing, consumer acceptance and trade acceptance. The key information areas that are emphasized by these two approaches vary significantly.

Consumer Acceptance Test-Marketing

As depicted by Exhibit 7–4, there are eight key information areas:

1. Consumer recognition of product characteristics of the product in question indicates that there will be a strong demand for it.

Important Areas of Key Information in Test Marketing	
Consumer Acceptance Test Marketing	*Trade Acceptance Test Marketing*
1. Consumer recognition of product characteristics	1. Convenience offered by the product
2. Consumer emphasis on these characteristics	2. Location within the store and the store itself
3. The degree of consumer loyalty created by test marketing	3. Product characteristics
4. Length of search time of the product by consumers	4. Price, displays and other promotional considerations
5. Brand image	5. Repeat purchases
6. Product image	6. Type of stores that should carry the product

7. Consumer attitude towards
   a. The physical product in general
   b. Its distribution
   c. Its promotion
	7. Trade attitude towards the product

8. Market profile for the new product (mainly consumer characteristics)	8. Marketing of competing products in the same area
	9. Market profile for the new product (mainly trade characteristics)

Exhibit 7–4 Consumer Acceptance versus Trade Acceptance

2. Consumer emphasis on these characteristics further indicates the strength of this potential demand. Eventually, these data will provide strong ammunition for advertising.

3. The degree of consumer loyalty created by test-marketing is a further indicator of the intensity of demand that this product is likely to enjoy once it reaches national markets.

4. The length of search time for the product on the part of consumers indicates the overall strength that the product is enjoying in the minds of consumers. If consumers are going out of their way for refills and searching for the product, then clearly it has strong powers to create product loyalty, which indicates the degree of success the proposed product is likely to enjoy.

5. The brand image for the new product indicates if the known brand will be a plus or minus factor. If the product has strong features and these are consistent with the brand image under which it is going to be marketed, this is a very strong combination.

6. Product image is the total picture that this product projects. If the product presents a strong image, it has a good chance for survival when it is marketed later on.

7. Consumer attitude measurement reinforces various product features and strengths. This is done toward the product in general, as well as its distribution and promotion.

8. Finally, market profile for the new product explores which individuals are most likely to buy the product.

As can be seen, consumer acceptance test-marketing can generate much data and, subsequently, some very important information that will help develop a good marketing plan. In the process, this activity also duplicates some of the data and perhaps some of the information as portions of the activity are likely to overlap and generate duplicate data.

Trade Acceptance Test-Marketing

Determining if the merchants, be they wholesalers or retailers, like a product will determine if it should be allowed to reach the national market and indicate the chances that it will be successful.

There are at least nine sets of data such a test could generate. Some of these will become critical information for marketing the product on a large scale later on.

1. Convenience offered by the product in terms of handling, storage, and shelf-life is a very critical consideration. Such considerations of convenience in handling can have a strong influence on the merchant's approval.

2. Location within the store and the location of the store itself make a substantial difference in determining the degree of acceptance that the new product will enjoy. Where the product is placed within a store impacts its sales, and consequently, it must be determined if location A is better than location B. Similarly, the product may not be suitable for an inner-city store or, perhaps, for a suburban store. Hence, the store location is important.

3. Product characteristics that appeal to merchants imply that the merchants will dwell on these features in pushing the product. The presence of these characteristics and their number are very critical in the push process. Merchants will never push a product if they themselves are not sold on it.

4. Trade acceptance test-marketing will yield particular data on the price of the product, how it may be displayed within the store, and

other promotional considerations such as posters, premiums, in-store discounts, free samples, and so forth.

5. Perhaps repeat purchases are the most critical indicators of whether the product will be successful. The merchants may provide such information as they repeat their orders during the test period.

6. Choosing the type of store that will carry the product is particularly critical. Whether a product should be marketed through, say, hardware stores, home improvement centers, or department stores is a major issue that is addressed effectively by a trade acceptance test.

7. All in all, detecting a comprehensive trade attitude toward the product is one of the key points of a trade acceptance test.

8. Merchants are in a position to provide input on the marketing of competing products. A trade acceptance test will provide some important data for marketing this product.

9. Finally, a trade acceptance test brings about a market profile indicating who in the marketplace will carry and, therefore, push this product.

As can be seen, consumer acceptance test-marketing is different from trade acceptance test-marketing. It is critical to reinforce the idea that in product-pull situations, consumers acceptance test-marketing is more beneficial, whereas in product-push situations, trade acceptance test-marketing is most appropriate.

MODERN TECHNIQUES OF EXPERIMENTAL DESIGNS

Experimental methods may be used for one particular variable at one time or for multiple variables. With the development of computers and highly sophisticated models, it has become possible to deal with a number of variables at the same time and to solve a problem for every variable simultaneously. Of course, such multivariate analysis is especially useful for social scientists, who find it is almost impossible to control all the variables at one time. But with computers, we can allow all the variables to vary and still solve problems as if it were possible to hold certain variables constant while the whole problem is solved for other variables.

Unfortunately, even if it is possible to conduct a complete experiment in marketing, the answer, unlike in the physical and biological sciences, is not usually absolute. If, for instance, it is found in an experiment that a new advertising campaign had stimulated sales, a statistical problem emerges as to the significance of the results. Similarly, the degree of causal relationship is an important question, because in marketing, it is not reasonable to expect a one-to-one causality. Often, multiple factors are responsible for one particular outcome. What are the relative roles of various factors in total causation? Problems such as these have forced statisticians to develop experimental designs that treat multiple variables and lend themselves to sophisticated measurement.

Three such designs that are discussed briefly here are randomized block designs, Latin square designs, and factorial analyses.

Randomized Block Designs

In this technique, multiple subjects are treated at multiple treatment levels. This is a standard experimental design in dealing with more than one variable. In experimental designs, quite often, the test units are not homogeneous and, hence, it is often possible that an uncontrolled variation may blur the results of the experiment. In this case, experimental units are grouped into blocks. It is assumed that within each block, units will be homogeneous in their response. Assume, for instance, an experiment to determine the best packaging design for XYZ shirts. The relative size of the retail outlets may confuse the picture, as three separate types of retail outlets for these shirts were to be used: specialty stores, department stores, and discount stores. Of the three types of packaging designs (treatment levels), the best one was to be determined.

Since the store type, which is an extraneous factor to the experiment, is nonetheless likely to influence the sales, it is necessary to remove this effect. This can be achieved by a so-called blocking process. Thus, since we do not have a completely homogeneous test unit in this case, the heterogeneity of the test unit is identified and it is stratified accordingly. Retail stores are stratified in three strata and randomization of the sample units is achieved within each block.

The experimental design is illustrated in Exhibit 7–5 where A, B, and C are three treatment levels (or packaging designs in this case). The

Treatment Levels			
Specialty stores	A	B	C
Department stores	A	B	C
Discount houses	A	B	C

Exhibit 7–5 Random Block Design

statistical technique used will enable researchers to determine the significantly better package design. By determining this significance, it is possible to decide whether one packaging design is significantly superior to others as the impact of the size of the store is neutralized.

Latin Squares

The Latin squares design is utilized in measuring the outcome of different levels of a particular variable while the effects of other variables are kept constant. Thus, the Latin squares design goes one step further than randomized blocks in that it blocks the effect of two or more variables simultaneously. This design enables the researcher to control, for instance, variations between cities that cannot be controlled in their selection. This type of design also becomes very important if the effectiveness of an effort such as a new advertising campaign is being tested.

Conventionally, one variable is presented in the rows of a table and another in the columns. While, for instance, the rows may represent a control for geographic variation in the form of different regions, the columns may stand for controlling competitive activity. Three levels of advertising or three different copies may be the subject of the design. It would imply that controls and treatments are independent of each other and that there is no interaction effect between them.

Assume that, in considering the package design for XYZ shirts, the size of the metropolitan area is also an important factor and that its impact should be blocked off. Then we have what may be called a 3×3 Latin square, which is depicted in Exhibit 7–6. As can be seen, the impact of the size of a metropolitan area can be detected by summarizing the columns, and the impact of the type of retail establishment, by summarizing the rows.

Thus, as can be seen, the Latin squares design reduces variation in an experiment and is somewhat similar to stratification in a sample survey, as it enables the researcher to control many independent variables simultaneously. The removal from the experiment of the effects of such

	Small Metropolitan Area	Medium Size Metropolitan Area	Large Metropolitan Area
Specialty Stores	A	B	C
Department Stores	B	C	A
Discount Stores	C	A	B

Exhibit 7–6 A 3 x 3 Latin Squares Design

variables as store size, time period, or region will necessarily yield better results. The most significant fact about the Latin squares design is that it does not treat each unit with each treatment; hence, it is much more economical than either random block or factorial designs.

Latin squares designs are employed in both store audits and accelerated store audits, in which case, preaudit periods are eliminated. Instead of changing one variable at a time and analyzing the impact through store audits, as in conventional experimentation, the Latin squares design permits substantial time savings. By means of an *analysis of variance* conducted on the results, the researcher is able to measure the relative importance of the different variables, such as geographic location, levels of advertising, and competitive activity. It is then possible to choose more effective policies and develop a better marketing mix.

The accelerated store audits, using Latin squares, differ from the general discussion only in the sense that the traffic in one of the observed stores is accelerated by the use of special devices such as price incentives. The degree of acceleration can be controlled by the offering. This approach necessitates a tighter control, which may mean an increase in the number of field personnel.

Factorial Designs

When it is reasonable to believe that the variables involved in a Latin squares design are interacting and, hence, exerting a special effect on the dependent variables, a full factorial design becomes necessary. The factorial design facilitates the measurement of both the main and interaction effects of two or more variables. Unlike the Latin squares, a full factorial design treats all subjects with all types of treatments included in the experiment.

Let us continue with our earlier example of XYZ shirts. For some reason it may be believed that the size of the metropolitan area, the type of retail outlet, and the type of package design interact. In other words, discount stores in large metropolitan areas may sell excessive amounts of type A packages. Hence, the Latin squares design of Exhibit 7–6 can no longer be used. Instead, a full factorial design, as shown in Exhibit 7–7, becomes necessary. This exhibit implies 3×3 blocks, which makes the factorial design much more involved and costly than the previous two designs. Let us assume, for simplicity, that we are still searching for the best package but have only two designs (A_1 and A_2), and two outlets (department stores and discount stores, B_1 and B_2, respectively).

This brief discussion has indicated that whenever the data are subject to an experimental or a sampling error, statistical methods offer the

		Small Metropolitan Areas M_1			Medium Size Metropolitan Areas M_2			Large Metropolitan Areas M_3		
Specialty stores	X	AXM_1	BXM_1	CXM_1	AXM_2	BXM_2	CXM_2	AXM_3	BXM_3	CXM_3
Department stores	Y	AYM_1	BYM_1	CYM_1	AYM_2	BYM_2	CYM_2	AYM_3	BYM_3	CYM_3
Discount stores	Z	AZM_1	BZM_1	CZM_1	AZM_2	BZM_2	CZM_2	AZM_3	BZM_3	CZM_3

Exhibit 7–7 A 3 x 3 Factorial Design

most efficient means of defining the appropriate test pattern and extracting meaningful information from the resultant data.

SUMMARY

This chapter deals with experimentation, with which the marketing decision maker should be familiar. Classical experiments require a *before* and *after* relationship in both *experimental* and *control* areas.

In this way, the decision maker may gain some understanding of causation. Because of the excessive costs, there has been a tendency to deviate from classical experimental situations. As a result, at least four types of pseudo-experiments have emerged: experiment-only, after-only, experiment-before and control-after, and test-marketing. These were discussed briefly in this chapter. Test-marketing is a very common practice. In this chapter, two different types of test-marketing were identified: consumer acceptance test-marketing and trade acceptance test-marketing.

In recent years, with the advancement of computer-assisted data generation, experimental designs have become more sophisticated and can now deal with multiple variables. Among these, three are discussed in this chapter: random blocks, Latin squares, and factorial designs.

REFERENCES

Blount, Steve. 1992. "Test Marketing: It's Just a Matter of Time." *Sales and Marketing Management*, March, 32–43.
Brennan, Leslie. 1988. "Special Supplement—Test Marketing." *Sales and Marketing Management*, March, 50–62.
Seeling, Pat. 1989. "All over the Map." *Sales and Marketing Management*, March, 58–64.
Stern, Aimee L. 1991. "Testing Goes Industrial." *Sales and Marketing Management*, March, 30–40.

8

Attitude Research

INTRODUCTION

The marketing decision maker needs to understand that the world is not simply black or white, yes or no. A prime example is consumer behavior, which is related to attitude. Thus, it is necessary to understand how attitudes are measured and used.

Consumer behavior is always triggered by the consumers' mental states. Attitudes are a part of these mental states, which guide individuals to structure how they perceive their environment and respond to it. Behind attitudes are three components that constitute overall attitude: cognitive, affective, and intention. Measuring attitude is particularly important for marketing researchers because a negative attitude never leads to a purchase, a repeat purchase, or positive networking for the company product or the brand. Without such knowledge, it is very difficult for marketing decision makers to allocate resources and decide whether to build, hold, harvest, or divest (Kotler 1994).

This chapter, first, explores the concept of attitude. Second, it presents a discussion on attitude measurement. Finally, it explores different types of attitude measurement and summarizes their usefulness for marketing decision makers.

THE CONCEPT OF ATTITUDE

Attitude is considered to have three key components: (1) cognitive, (2) affective, and (3) intention. These are illustrated in Exhibit 8–1.

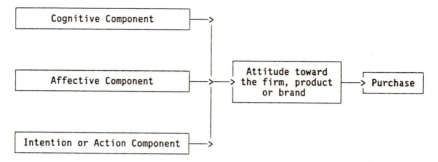

Exhibit 8–1 Components of Attitude

Cognitive Component

The cognitive component is the knowledge component. Individuals, through their systems of perception, gather sensory data and, within their brains, process them into information. Part of the sensory data is generated through interaction with others, and the other part is generated through the individual's own attempts to gather data and generate information. Naturally, the knowledge component can be measured and influenced with some degree of certainty.

Affective Component

The affective component relates readily to likes and dislikes. It is an emotional component. Emotions are partly related to the individual's psyche and partially to his or her cultural background, making this aspect of attitude difficult to measure.

Intention Component

The intention component is also known as the action component. From a marketing perspective, this is the most important component of overall attitude. Perhaps more than the other two, this component indicates whether the consumer is likely to buy the product or the service in question.

Attitudes are qualitative information and, as such, they need to be quantified and measured. Unless the data can somehow be ordered or arranged in meaningful patterns, attitudes cannot be measured. Attitudinal research is based on this measurement criterion to provide marketing decision makers with an indication of the intensity of the feelings and thinking behind the attitudes. An important aspect of attitudes is their intensity. If there is a high-intensity attitude toward buying a product rather than a low-intensity attitude toward not buying it, it is clear that the marketing decision maker needs to launch a proactive marketing plan in order to reach and penetrate the market. Thus, attitudes need to be measured in terms of both strengths and direction (Weiers 1984).

Because attitudes have different intensity levels, it is necessary to generate data on these levels. In order to measure such qualitative phenomena as attitudes and their levels of intensity, attitude scales are used. The four most commonly used scalar tools are the *nominal, ordinal, interval,* and *ratio* scales. Exhibit 8–2 illustrates the key features of these scales and their typical areas of application.

Nominal Scales

The nominal scale provides the simplest means of transforming data into a symbolic format. This type of scale actually does not permit a rank ordering of individual bits of data but instead allows the information to be arrayed in an "either-or" format. Thus, favorable attitudes on the part of consumers may be coded "1" and unfavorable attitudes, "2." To provide a further example, telephone subscribers holding credit card

Scale	Measurement Characteristics	Basic Empirical Operation	Typical Areas of Application
Nominal	Objects are either identical or different	Determination of equality	All kinds of classifications (by sex, region, social class)
Ordinal or Rank Order	Objects are greater or smaller	Determination of size differences	Rankings in terms of intensity
Interval	Intervals between adjacent ranks are equal	Measurement of differences or equalities	Index numbers, other types of scales (such as temperature)
Ratio	The presence of zero point makes it possible to measure magnitudes in absolute terms	Determination of equality or inequality of ratios	Sales, incomes, variety of units developed by the scales, costs

SOURCE: Adopted and revised from Stevens, S. S. (1946), "On the Theory of Scales of Measurement," *Science*, June 7, 677-680. Aaker, David A. and George S. Day (1990), *Marketing Research*, New York: John Wiley & Sons.

Exhibit 8–2 Scales: Their Characteristics and Their Use

privileges may be assigned one code and non–credit card holders, another.

.The basic empirical operation underlying the nominal scale is the determination of equality. In other words, by means of this scale, two large groups can be established, with all objects or items in the first group equal to each other but with the items in the two respective groups being opposite each other, at least with respect to the characteristic being measured.

Ordinal Scales

Ordinal scales are the simplest scales that are used to any large extent in marketing research. This type of scale does permit rank ordering, but the various ranks established by this scale are relative rather than absolute. While the numbers assigned by means of an ordinal scale ordinarily have symmetrical intervals (1, 2, 3, 4, 5; 2, 4, 8, 16, 32, 64; etc.), these intervals do not carry over to the data being measured. Having equal intervals is *not* a characteristic of ordinal scales. An ordinal scale, in a sense, is like an elastic tape measure that is being stretched unevenly. The scale positions, as indicated by the numbers on the tape, are in a clearly defined order, but the numbers do not provide a definite indication of the distance between any two points.

Interval Scales

Interval scales permit rank ordering and also allow for the measurement of the intervals between each item. In this type of scale, the intervals are of equal size. Thus, on a scale numbered 1 to 10, item 6 is the same distance from item 5 as is item 4.

Ratio Scales

The ratio scale, like the interval scale, permits rank ordering and contains intervals that are equal in size. The one great advantage of the ratio scale is that it also contains a zero position and, as its name implies, permits the establishment of ratios among the values being measured. Whereas the interval scale only permits relationships (albeit exact) to be established among items, ratio scales also permit absolute values to be assigned.

A twelve-inch ruler is a good example of a ratio scale. Not only is it possible to say that the values 3 and 6 are three units apart, we can also say that six inches is twice as much as three inches. Ratio scales are quite common in the physical sciences, but because of the imprecise nature of marketing data, they are relatively insignificant in market research.

If we want to determine the intensity of an attitude, two different approaches can be used. The first involves measuring the intensity of the attitude by itself. This situation calls for attitude-rating scales, which scales offer itemized category scales such as, very satisfied—quite satisfied—somewhat satisfied—not at all satisfied, or comparative scales such as, very superior—neutral—very inferior. These are balanced, and they provide a range within the constraints of the topic being explored.

The second approach is to compare the intensity with a number of other intensities. The scales that are used in this case are called rank order scales.

Rank order scales ask the respondent to arrange a set of objects based on a specified common denominator (Aaker & Day 1990). The specified denominator may be product features, advertisements on the basis of their appeal, and so forth. In other words, these scales attempt to determine how respondents rank alternatives. Consider, for instance:

> Where do you receive information about XYZ Company? Please rank the following sources, with (1) being most important, and so on.
>
> _____ a. Advertisements
>
> _____ b. Radio announcements
>
> _____ c. TV commercials
>
> _____ d. Other professionals
>
> _____ e. Friends
>
> _____ f. Other (please specify)_____.

Obviously different variables or factors can be the common criterion here, such as getting information about the company or the importance of a product and the like. Rank order scales are ordinal scales, and their use is limited in regard to generating new information through the use of sophisticated data analysis techniques. However, a more advanced version of the rank order scale is the *constant-sum scale*. These scales ask the respondents to divide a fixed amount of rating points (typically 100) among various alternatives.

Aaker and Day (1990, 281) used the following illustration:

> Please divide 100 points among the following characteristics so the division reflects the relative importance of each characteristic to you in the selection of a health care plan.
>
> _____ Ability to choose a doctor
>
> _____ Extent of coverage provided

_____ Quality of medical care

_____ Monthly cost of the plan

_____ Distance to clinic or doctor from your home

_____ Other (please specify) _____

Unlike the typical rank order scales, constant-sum scales, although not scientifically proven, are considered to be interval scales (Aaker & Day 1990). Hence, more sophisticated statistical analyses can be used in processing the data generated by these scales.

In general, ranking scales do not have the sensitivity of rating scales in determining the intensity of the attitude. However, in most marketing-related attitudinal studies, the subject matter is multifaceted and complex. Therefore, attitudes need to be measured, and with more than one overall attitude measurement. Thus, they are measured with multiple attitude scales that measure different aspects of the phenomenon in question. There are a number of different types of rating scales, but only two are very popular among marketing researchers: (1) Likert scales and (2) semantic differential scales.

Likert Scales

These scales ask respondents to indicate their reaction to certain stimuli in terms of their degree of agreement or disagreement. Exhibit 8–3 illustrates an attempt to measure the overall attitude toward World Gym by exploring the intensity of the respondents' like or dislike of a number of its attributes.

As seen in the exhibit, a number of statements indicating various attributes are first developed, and then, typically, a five-point rating scale is used. It has been stated that seven- and nine-point scales are too complicated for typical respondents (Aaker & Day 1990). The lack of an outlet other than registering a reaction on the intensity of an opinion or the opinion itself is a problem in these scales. This means that "no opinion" or "don't know" cannot be registered. A further problem is related to wording, as words used in these scales may not be clear to the population as a whole. Finally, there is always the problem of including all the important components or features of the phenomenon in question. For instance, an attitude toward a product and its features may be measured by respondents who may be inclined to buy another product because of convenience.

Questions about World Gym:

		Strongly Agree	Agree	Neutral	Disagree	Strongly Disagree
(a)	World Gym is a nice place to exercise in.	□	□	□	□	□
(b)	World Gym has a very good atmosphere.	□	□	□	□	□
(c)	Equipment in the World Gym is state of the art.	□	□	□	□	□
(d)	Equipment in the World Gym is well maintained.	□	□	□	□	□
(e)	There is always professional advice and guidance.	□	□	□	□	□
(f)	World Gym's location is very good for many of its members.	□	□	□	□	□
(g)	World Gym has reasonable membership rates.	□	□	□	□	□
(h)	World Gym promotes itself well.	□	□	□	□	□
(i)	All in all World Gym is a nice place to be a member of.	□	□	□	□	□

Exhibit 8–3 The Likert Scale Part of a Questionnaire

Semantic Differential Scale

Perhaps the most popular tool of attitudinal research in marketing is the semantic differential scale. This procedure is used to describe the specifics of a set of adjectives that are likely to represent a person's, store's, brand's, or product's image, as seen by the respondents. It is particularly useful in comparing competing images of different stores, brands, or products.

The technique involves showing the respondents a series of bipolar adjectives relative to the object. By placing a response within each pair of polar adjectives, the respondent enables the researcher to probe into the content and intensity of the stimuli.

Typically, in order to evaluate the attitude toward the object, there may be some fifteen to twenty-five semantic differential scales. Examples of bipolar adjectives dealing with a store image are as follows:

traditional—modern

static—dynamic

classic merchandise—up-to-date fashions

friendly—unfriendly

These bipolar adjectives can be presented in the form of monopolar or bipolar scales.

Monopolar scales will use such terms as *traditional—not traditional,* and bipolar scales, such terms as *traditional—modern.* If the adjective is a good description of the object, the respondent will choose the endpoint, whereas if the adjective is not a good description, the respondent will choose the midpoint (if the scale is bipolar) or the other extreme (if it is monopolar).

In order for semantic-differential scales to be effective, four conditions must to be met.

1. It is necessary to make sure that all the most important attributes are included and described to respondents in familiar words.
2. The negative or unfavorable extreme has to be on the right side some of the time and on the left at other times to avoid a "halo" effect by encouraging the respondent to select one set of extremes only (e.g., the right side).
3. In dealing with different attributes, a group of variables is used. There are groups of scales dealing with these variables, in which these variable categories are treated as interval scales, allowing group mean values to be established (Aaker & Day 1990).
4. In determining an overall attitude through semantic-differential scales measuring attitude, the key attributes need to be assumed to be of equal weights. If there is any reason to assume that in the World Gym, for example, membership rates are more important than the equipment, the scales need to be weighted. Such techniques are known as multiattribute attitude scales.

ATTITUDES AND MARKETING DECISION MAKERS

The cognitive, affective, and action components of attitudes imply how individuals' attitudes develop and the role that marketing can play. If cognitive learning and affective values do not exist, consumers are not likely to buy the company's products. Thus, the marketing decision maker can learn how attitudes are formed and influenced.

One of the most important features of semantic differential scales, for instance, is that they could lead to profile analysis as shown in Exhibit 8–4. Three wines are compared to each other and their profiles are analyzed by conducting research based on semantic-differential scales. The exhibit illustrates the results of such an attitude study. The profiles of these three wines indicate that they are quite different.

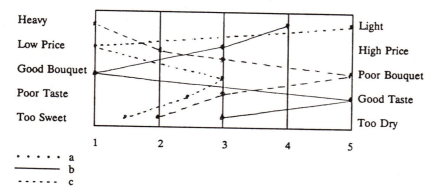

Exhibit 8–4   Profile Analysis of Three Wines

Brand a is a low-priced light wine with somewhat acceptable bouquet. Its taste is not considered to be good (a score of about 2.3 on a 5-point scale) and is too sweet.

Brand b is a relatively light, medium-priced wine. It has a very good bouquet and very good taste. It is neither too sweet nor too dry.

Brand c is a very heavy wine with a poor bouquet. Its taste is somewhat acceptable, and it is relatively sweet.

On the basis of the profiles presented in Exhibit 8–4 the company can easily decide if these wines are fulfilling the needs of the identified target markets and if there should be some changes in marketing plans, including elimination of these products and introduction of other products. Semantic-differential scales can be much longer and provide valuable additional information that can be used by the company.

Attitude research is an important managerial tool with which consumer-oriented, proactive companies can make early adjustments. Similarly, this type of research is extremely important in developing and changing marketing plans.

Exhibit 8–5 illustrates how attitude research can be used in different stages of the product life cycle. In addition to the standard four stages of the product life cycle, I maintain that when a product is at the conceptual or developmental stages, attitude research can be used to predict the expected product success (Samli, Palda, & Barker 1987).

Exhibit 8–5 points out that, at the introductory stage, attitude research can help predict the potential market share for a new product. Similarly, such research can also help improve a product by focusing on the consumer reaction toward it. The second stage in the life cycle is

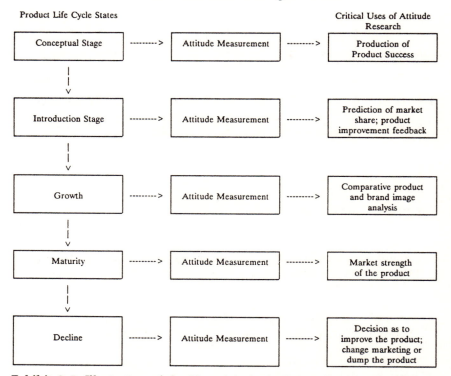

Exhibit 8–5 Illustration of the Use of Attitude Research in Product-Related Marketing Decisions

growth. Here, attitude research needs to generate information regarding competitive performance of the product. Changes in its image are a critical early indicator of how a product is likely to perform.

Maturity is the third stage. Attitude research at this stage can determine market strength and consumer loyalty to the product. Such knowledge can be helpful in maintaining or revising the marketing plan, as needed. Finally, the fourth stage is decline. At this point, the company has to make decisions to improve the product or change the marketing plan. The other alternative at this stage is to drop the product. Attitude research provides valuable information regarding these areas.

SUMMARY

This chapter, first, presents a brief discussion of the concept of attitude. Then it points out that attitudes can be measured by scales. Scales are defined as nominal, ordinal, interval, and ratio. The simplest is the nominal, while the most sophisticated is the ratio scale. As the scaling technique becomes more sophisticated, it becomes subject to more rigorous statistical analyses and, hence, can generate more significant and sophisticated information.

Scales in a functional sense are categorized into ranking and rating scales. Most scales used in marketing research are rating scales. Among these, two are extremely popular in marketing circles: Likert scales and semantic-differential scales, both of which are versatile tools for marketing purposes. They have strengths and weaknesses but have nonetheless proved to be quite useful. The chapter finally presents a discussion about the use of attitude research in product management discussions.

REFERENCES

Aaker, David A., and George S. Day. 1990. *Marketing Research.* New York: John Wiley and Sons.

Kotler, Philip. 1994. *Marketing Management.* Englewood Cliffs, NJ: Prentice-Hall.

Samli, A. Coskun, Christian Palda, and Tansu Barker. 1987. "Toward a Mature Marketing Concept." *Sloan Management Review,* Winter, 45–51.

Stevens, S. S. 1946. "On the Theory of Scales of Measurement." *Science,* June 7, 677–80.

Weiers, Ronald M. 1984. *Marketing Research: A Structure for Decisions.* Reading, MA: Addison-Wesley.

9

Motivation Research

INTRODUCTION

Motivation research is a critical component of consumer behavior databases.[1] However, it is not readily quantifiable, and therefore, most researchers who are trained to be quantitative are hesitant to be involved in this type of *qualitative* research. Additionally, motivation research reaches out and deals with human motivation, which involves probing the subconscious. However, the subconscious is not a standard area of research for the corporate marketing researchers, who tend to be comfortable with computers and oriented toward quantitative data.

The marketing decision maker must realize that, at least in part, consumer behavior is related to the subconscious; hence, it is critical that this part of consumer behavior be explained. Motivation, whether consciously or subconsciously triggered, is the reason behind behavior (Hawkins, Best, & Coney 1989), and hence must be understood and dealt with for successful marketing, particularly in the consumer market.

This chapter deals with the concept of motivation, explaining how motives can be identified and researched and the techniques used in motivation research. It is critical to include this aspect of research.

MOTIVATION AND QUALITATIVE RESEARCH

In the 1940s and 1950s, qualitative research, and particularly motivation research, was widespread (Packard 1957). Sampson (1985, 69) stated:

1. Most of this chapter is based on Samli and Wilkinson 1987.

Qualitative research grew out of the meeting, in the 1940s, of refugee Freudians and neo-Freudians seeking to apply some of the principles of psychoanalysis in a marketing context, and the pollsters, seeking to extend their measurement of behavior and attitudes, on a large scale, to the same field.

In the United States, the second group quickly took over and emphasized the measurement of attitudes. This aspect of behavior, therefore, has become better known and clearly has been better researched (see Chapter 8 for details). During the past three decades in the United States, attitude research made significant strides on both methodological and measurement fronts. On the other hand, motivation research appeared to be dormant at best (Samli & Wilkinson 1987). Only attention seekers, such as Key (1973), put nominal amount of emphasis to it under his rubric of "subliminal seduction." During the same period, however, a new wave of motivation research emerged in Europe and is still going strong (Bigant & Rickebusch 1985; Schlackman 1984; Samuels 1984).

Understanding consumers' motives behind their purchase behavior enables marketers to predict consumer behavior. Understanding behavior patterns also facilitates the possibilities of intercepting and modifying them. In attempting to predict consumer behavior, the prices behind the behavior patterns are analyzed. On the American scene, because of quantitative expediency, attitudes have been singled out as the sole force behind behavior. As attitude research has become increasingly sophisticated, many new and powerful techniques emerged.

Perhaps the most critical problem with attitude research is that the information that is obtained exists at the conscious awareness level. It is questionable whether consumers always behave consciously and are always aware of the forces causing their behavior. Thus, it may be erroneous to attribute behavior entirely, or even primarily, to attitudes and to analyze the whole process at the conscious level alone. The subconscious or unconscious levels of human behavior, which form and manipulate motives, may not manifest themselves as attitudes all at once. Furthermore, even if attitudes were to reflect all the conscious residual of motives, they still show only their direction and would not explain their origins. Thus, attitudes may not be totally adequate to explain variables of behavior and therefore, they are not good predictors of behavior (Samli & Wilkinson 1987).

It is posited here that the forces behind the behavior are organized in the form of a hierarchy and that parts of this hierarchy are located in the subconscious. If we want to understand behavior, the subconscious portion of the hierarchy of forces behind consumer behavior needs to be put in proper perspective and understood. Without this understanding, an effective prediction of consumer behavior is virtually impossible because it will be impossible to comprehend it fully (Samli & Wilkinson 1987).

Europeans have understood the importance of this gap in American consumer databases and have busied themselves in developing new and varied techniques of motivation research, which they have termed "qualitative research" (Cooper & Branthwaite 1977; Wicken 1977; Fleury 1984).

EARLY MOTIVATION RESEARCH EFFORTS

As Green and Carmone (1970) maintained, when the reasons behind the purchases are known, future purchase projections are strengthened. Strong proponents of motivation research, who called it a qualitative science (Gottlieb 1985), maintained that the psychological reasons behind given behavior patterns can be determined only by using motivation research. There is a rich literature of this type, which came about during the late 1950s and some examples of which include:

A California prune growers' association wanted to know what caused people's negative attitudes towards prunes and how to make those attitudes more positive (Packard 1957).

The finding that baking a cake is a creative act for a woman, perhaps as a substitute for child bearing, helped to explain why cake mixes with the instructions "do not add milk, just water" were not very successful. General Mills' Bisquick therefore instructed consumers to add fresh eggs in order to return the creativity element to the housewife (Packard 1957).

Once motivation research found out that Rye-Crisp crackers were not perceived by stout people as a diet food, Rye-Crisp was repositioned as a cocktail snack (Gustafson 1958).

Motivation research indicated that cutting the price for cosmetics may be an ineffective approach. Consumers of lipstick and shampoos stated that for them, low price indicated a low-quality product, which might even be harmful to the user (Gustafson 1958).

The Japanese textile industry wanted to know accurately the views of the American public about the industry and its products (Gustafson 1958).

A manufacturer of laxatives wanted to know why sales were weak in certain markets and what advertising appeals would be most effective (Gardner 1959).

By the mid-1960s, however, motivation research had come to a near halt. The cause can be traced to the emergence of what might be called the "school of management by the numbers." The advent of more empirical methodologies that accompanied the rapidly spreading use of computers created a management style that relied heavily, if not exclusively, on the quantitative manipulation of numerical inputs. This emphasis on numbers fostered the growth of attitudinal research, which is substantially more measurable and quantifiable than motivation research. The rise of attitudinal research closely paralleled the development of a very rich variety of multivariate techniques (Kendall 1968, 1975; Cooley & Lohnes 1971). As attitudinal research emphasized the analysis of scalar data through multivariate techniques, it paralyzed the growth of motivation research. Thus, a kind of "quantitative myopia" prevented marketing research from looking beyond conscious awareness into the subconscious to find quantitative techniques for dealing with the conscious proliferated and became increasingly esoteric. It then became difficult even to acknowledge the role of the subconscious in consumer behavior.

THE SUBCONSCIOUS AND CONSUMER BEHAVIOR

Consumer purchase behavior is a series of responses to a series of pressures caused by a series of internal forces. Exhibit 9–1 illustrates this concept. Individual internal forces are precipitated, molded, and reinforced by various environmental factors or cues. These forces lead to pressures and frustrations on the part of the consumer. These pressures and frustrations will not be relieved until a purchase takes place. This process can be seen in greater detail as Exhibit 9–2 is examined. Two separate hierarchies are presented in the exhibit: (1) a hierarchy of forces and (2) a hierarchy of responses. The hierarchies are conceived to be moving upward from the broadest, most fundamental, and general to the narrowest, most derivative, and most specific. The forces hierarchy, depicting the triggering factors that cause a response, begins with basic drive forces that are completely undifferentiated, such as "hunger" (the drive for food), which triggers a need response for an undifferentiated object: Any kind of food will do—whatever is most

Exhibit 9–1 Purchase and Its Antecedents

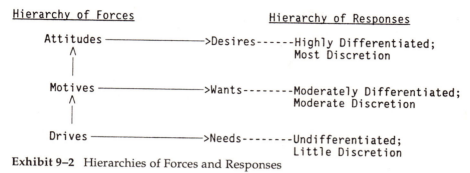

Exhibit 9–2   Hierarchies of Forces and Responses

convenient and economical; this is a "food as fuel" response. At the motive level, the want responses are somewhat more differentiated and therefore discretionary, and most often specify a product class, such as candy bars: Any candy bar will do, but the motive is now channeling the hunger drive into wanting some kind of sweet confection. At the most specific and discretionary level, attitudes toward individual brands of candy bars have channeled the want for a candy bar into the highly specific desire for, say, a Snickers bar. Neither wants nor desires are directly related to survival, although they may be the indirect consequences of primary drives. The individual, therefore, develops wants and desires that are increasingly selective and that must be fulfilled with increasing selectivity. In a consumer behavior model, all needs, wants, and desires are fulfilled, directly or indirectly, by purchases and their subsequent consumption or use.

In order to understand consumer behavior well and be successful in predicting it, the hierarchy of forces must be understood. As seen in Exhibit 9–2, the hierarchy moves from very general and basic to very idiosyncratic and specific. It is also apparent that it parallels Maslow's hierarchy (Kotler 1994), according to which individuals strive to move up from satisfying their basic physiological needs to self-actualization, the highest level in the hierarchy. An individual cannot self-actualize by satisfying basic needs derived directly from the drives. Satisfying basic needs by following drives would enable the individual to survive, but nothing more than that. Self-actualization takes place when the combined pressures of drives, motives, and attitudes lead to behavior that expresses itself in an idiosyncratic and discretionary purchase activity. Although purchase activity related directly to drives and motives may occur, such purchases are not likely to bring the individual closer to self-actualization.

Regardless of how discretionary the purchases, once the individual is beyond the basic need (or survival) level, the forces behind his or her actions have both conscious and subconscious components (Sampson 1985). While structured interviews and attitudinal research reach the conscious level of consumer behavior, motivation research, or qualitative research, as it is termed in Europe, deals with the subconscious. In describing the "new" qualitative research, Cooper and Branthwaite (1977) offered the following explanation: As we go further down [into the subconscious], obtaining responses by structured interviewing becomes progressively more difficult. And, by the same token, responses to qualitative interviewing becomes more reliable because these interviews are better able to cope with private feelings, irrationalities, 'illogical' behavior or repressed attitudes. Thus, it is implied that the subconscious should be examined and understood separately because at this level there are the possibilities of having irrationality, illogical behavior, and attitudes that are repressed at the conscious level. It is quite likely that the transition from subconscious to conscious levels cannot be understood well by researching only the conscious. Early motivation research studies relating to instant coffee (Haire 1950), mouthwashes, air conditioners, and insurance (Packard 1957) are all indicative of such irrationalities or repressed attitudes. Certainly, less-than-rational motives cannot possibly lead to the development of entirely rational attitudes. It is, therefore, extremely important to explore the subconscious in order to better understand motives.

This point is illustrated in Exhibit 9–3. In attempting to sell bottled water, motivation research may identify any one of the three motives: safety, health, or status. As seen in the exhibit, each of the three attitudes can lead to the development of an appropriate marketing strategy. However, if behind these attitudes there is a subconscious motive, the marketing strategies are not likely to work. The subconscious motive of fear of early death needs to be incorporated into the marketing strategy by emphasizing any of the other strategies (whichever is appropriate), along with long life or health leading to long life. In Europe, there has been a resurgence of qualitative research that deals primarily with motives (Fleury 1984, 1985). In pursuit of such research, a number of new techniques have been developed.

One of the emerging concepts in qualitative research is that even though human beings are unique as individuals, they are irretrievably molded in the common pattern of a certain culture or subculture in which they were born and reared. This means, for instance, that a brand not only gives functional satisfaction or psychological imagery but also conveys a great deal of meaning to individuals in the form of fundamental social values instituted into people by their cultures (Collins 1991).

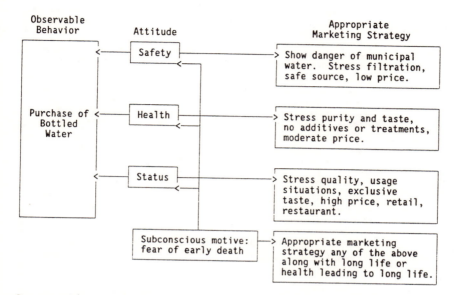

Source: Adopted and revised from Hawkins, Del, Roger J. Best and Kenneth A. Coney (1989), *Consumer Behavior*, Homewood, IL: BPI-Irwin, p. 355.

Exhibit 9–3 Conscious and Subconscious Motives

NEW TECHNIQUES OF MOTIVATION RESEARCH

Cooper and Lannon (1983) presented a comprehensive, though not exhaustive, list of techniques as vehicles for tapping intuition and the unconscious: (1) role-playing, (2) personal analogies, (3) direct analogies, (4) symbolic analogies, (5) fantasy solutions/ future scenarios, (6) psycho-doodle/psycho-drawing/psycho-lumps, (7) adjectivization, (8) personification, (9) projective techniques, and (10) group conflict/competition. Seven more techniques were added to this list: (11) collage (de Souza 1984), (12) photo sorting (Heylen 1984b), (13) play-oneiric tests (Frontori, Pogliana, & Spataro 1984), (14) the triangular interview (Fleury 1984), (15) transactional analysis (Blackstone & Holmes 1984), (16) libido theory (Heylen 1984a, 1984b), and (17) semiotics/semiology (Krief 1984).

Of these techniques, eight are considered to be lesser known but are currently receiving special attention in Europe (Sampson 1985). These techniques will be briefly but critically discussed in the remainder of this chapter: (1) psycho-drawing, (2) collage, (3) photo-sorting, (4) play-oneiric tests, (5) the triangular interview, (6) transactional analy-

TECHNIQUE	APPROACH	IMPORTANT STRENGTH	KEY WEAKNESS
Psycho-drawing	Quick sketching that relates to perceptions, aspirations, etc.	Being able to illustrate concepts and meanings that people cannot articulate.	Reluctance on the part of those who don't draw well.
Collage	Giving respondents a pile of magazines and asking them to cut out the pictures, drawings, and words that express their feelings.	Effective in describing brands, products, and symbols.	Expression of feelings and views is limited to the availability of materials.
Photo-sorting	Associating a series of pre-sorted, scaled, and standardized photographs to a series of products and brands.	Pre-standardized photos provide a good control for specific dimensions to be explored.	Same problem experienced in collage, only more serious.
Play-oneiric Tests	A play technique that is related to an imaginary dream associated with brand, product, store, etc.	In markets where products or brands are functionally similar, they are symbolically positioned and distinguished.	Extremely complex interpretation procedures.
Triangular Interview	An actor, a respondent, and an interviewer follow a scenario for a communication check.	Eliminates the desire to give the "right" answer and therefore built-in biases.	Difficult to implement.
Transactional Analysis	Analyzing the exchange between individuals or between consumer and brands on the basis of established "T.A." techniques.	Brings psychoanalytic and behavioristic theories together.	Needs highly skilled professional to implement.
Libido Theory	Combining psychoanalysis and social biology to explain the deeper dimensions of behavior.	Eliminates ill-conceived symbology.	Very complex technique is new and difficult to use.
Semiotics/ Semiology	The science of signs and symbols in society uses the whole field of verbal and visual communication.	Distinction between denotative and connotative meanings of each symbol provides a stronger brand analysis.	Too new and complex; technique needs special expertise.

Exhibit 9–4   A Comparative Analysis of Eight Techniques

sis, (7) libido theory, and (8) semiotics/semiology. (See also Exhibit 9–4.)

Psycho-drawing

This technique revolves around "quick sketching" in small groups. Drawings are analyzed on the basis of material, shapes, colors, tone, and so forth, in order to assess perceptions, aspirations, values, and similar phenomena. Typically, respondents are asked to explain their drawings in considerable detail to the group. Although the technique is designed to overcome reluctance to draw, some remnants of this reluctance seem to remain (de Souza 1984).

Collage

The collage technique involves giving respondents a pile of magazines and asking them to cut out those pictures, drawings, and words that express their feelings about the product, brand, store, and so forth. It is a technique that does overcome drawing problems and taps into a vast range of symbols in order to determine how products and brands are perceived (de Souza 1984). The materials are still limited, however, and may restrict the ability of some respondents to express themselves.

Photo Sorting

Heylen's (1984a, 1984b) psychodynamic approach is the core of this technique. It requires a set of photographs that symbolize people (pictures for physiognomic analysis, homes, automobiles, etc.). These pictures are standardized and sorted on the basis of certain dimensions that are determined in advance. Heylen (1984a) called this procedure *implicit conative dynamics*. The technique has the same problem as the collage technique, only more pronounced.

Play-oneiric Tests

Frontori, Pogliana, and Spataro (1984) described this technique by explaining how a psychoanalytic theory of language may be applied to basic motivation research and communication studies (Sampson 1985). The technique goes beneath the cognitive structure by helping to determine the affective-symbolic structures and the emotional substance of the images. The approach is particularly appropriate for products or services that are functionally similar and need to be differentiated or positioned in a distinctively competitive manner. The respondents are asked to describe the dream of an individual who comes in contact with the object in question. The interpretation is very complex and takes place in multiple levels.

The Triangular Interview

This technique is designed to avoid the demand and experimenter biases generated by a respondent seeking to give the "right" answer in the context of the interviewer's presupposed knowledge of the subject matter (Sampson 1985). Fleury (1984) explained that by this method, the desire to give the right answer is replaced by the desire to understand the problem. The technique is rather difficult to implement because of unexpected additional interactions among the interviewer, actor, and respondent.

Transactional Analysis

Developed by Berne (1973), this technique, which was adapted to marketing research by Blackstone and Holmes (1984), combines psychoanalytic and behavioristic theories. According to this technique, the exchange between individuals, between consumer and brand, or between consumer and advertising is an act of recognition (termed a "stroke"). Strokes can be physical, psychological, or symbolic, and they can also be either positive or negative. The technique provides a deeper understanding of such aspects of marketing as brand choice, brand imagery, and brand communication. Its use in marketing is very new and complex as its implementation is highly technical and requires well-trained personnel (Klein 1983).

Libido Theory

This extremely original approach was developed by Heylen (1984a, 1984b) and brings together social biology and psychoanalysis. According to Heylen, the technique was meant to develop a theory and methodology to explain the deeper dimensions of consumer behavior (1984a). The theory takes a strong anticognitivist stance and maintains that there is a conative dimension that deals with subconscious or unconscious values and aspirations. The technique revolves around extensive empirical testing based on a complex set of visually presented concrete symbols. The extreme complexity of the technique makes it difficult to use.

Semiotics/Semiology

This technique has been given particular attention in France (Krief 1984). Based on the linguistic theories of de Saussure (1974), semiotics studies the whole field of verbal and visual communications in a society. There are two levels of meaning for signs and symbols, *denotative* and *connotative*. Denotative stands for the explicit literal meaning of the sign, and *connotative* refers to the implicit underlying meaning (Barthes 1967; Sampson 1985). The technique dwells upon the concept of codes being central to the formation and understanding of messages, which is very culture-specific. Krief (1984) used semiotics to develop a "communications audit" that evaluates supply (i.e., the product, promotional, and communications mixes) and demand (i.e., consumers' needs and expectations). Analyzing consumers' motivations and the semiotics of communication simultaneously provides a powerful orientation for researching the subconscious. This also is a very complex technique that requires a high level of expertise to implement.

IMPLICATIONS FOR THE
MARKETING RESEARCHER

From the perspective of the marketing decision maker, this chapter must be a major eye-opener. It is clear that there is additional information to be generated from qualitative research that may be critical to the decision-making process of the firm and subsequently, to its well-being in the marketplace. It must be realized that typical marketing researchers are not trained in the qualitative research area. Because this type of research is particularly difficult to quantify, they may be particularly hesitant to explore this research avenue. Hence, marketing decision makers may have to go out of their way to generate such research and the information that it develops.

SUMMARY

As seen in this chapter, motivation research is alive and thriving in Europe. Once North American marketing researchers break through the artificial barriers imposed by managing with numbers only and relieve their consequent "quantitative myopia," it will be possible to take up the legitimate study of the subconscious where it was left off. This is not to assert that qualitative and quantitative research activities are substitutes for one another so much as that they are complementary. It seems that there is much merit in delving into the subconscious for a better understanding of behavior and in order to predict it more accurately.

In the past, the biggest problem with motivation research has been measurement. It has been claimed by more quantitatively oriented scientists that this type of research is extremely subjective and does not lend itself to scientific quantification (Rothwell 1955; Scriven 1958; Schiffman & Kanuk 1992). It is maintained here, however, that under normal circumstances, individuals who are of similar socioeconomic and cultural backgrounds and have undergone the same types of experiences will display similar motivational patterns. In other words, the motivational characteristics of ghetto youths will be similar to one another and significantly different from those of, say, Amish farmers or Mormon women living in the suburbs of Salt Lake City. If this premise can be accepted, then the use of any and all of the techniques discussed here becomes valid as long as the samples are tightly specified. Much needs to be done to test the applicability of this position. However, the question must be raised as to whether North American marketing researchers are depriving themselves by ignoring a very important component of consumer behavior, the subconscious? The answer on our part is a very strong "yes," and we hope that more attention will be paid to this very important and exciting area.

REFERENCES

Barthes, R. 1967. *Elements of Semiology*. London: Cape.
Berne, E. 1973. *What Do You Say after You Say Hello?* New York: Bantam Books.
Bigant, J., and Y. Rickebusch. 1985. "Marketing Research in France." *European Research* 13(1) (January): 4–11.
Blackstone, M., and M. Holmes. 1984. "The Use of Transactional Analysis in the Development of a New Brand's Personality." In *Proceedings*, 105–18. Athens, Greece: ESOMAR Seminar on New Product Development.
Collins, Leslie F. 1991. "Everything Is True, But in a Different Sense: A New Perspective on Qualitative Research." *Journal of the Market Research Society* (January): 31–38.
Cooley, W. W., and P. R. Lohnes. 1971. *Multivariate Data Analysis*. New York: John Wiley and Sons.
Cooper, P., and A. Branthwaite. 1977. "Qualitative Technology: New Perspectives on Measurement and Meaning through Qualitative Research." In *Proceedings*, 79–92. Brighton, U.K.: MRS Conference.
Cooper, P., and J. Lannon. 1983. "Humanistic Advertising: A Holistic Cultural Perspective." *International Journal of Advertising* 2:195–213.
de Saussure, F. 1974. *Course in General Linguistics*. London: Fontana. (originally published 1915)
de Souza, M. 1984. "For a Better Understanding of Individuals: Non-Verbal Approaches." In *Proceedings*, 163–76. Copenhagen, Denmark: EMAC/ESOMAR Symposium on Methodological Advances in Marketing Research Theory and Practice.
Fleury, P. 1984. "New Qualitative Studies." In *Proceedings*, 629–47. Rome, Italy: ESOMAR Congress, September.
———. 1985. "Market Research in France: The Empire of Qualitative Studies." *European Research* (April): 13–17.
Frontori, L., A. Pogliana, and B. Spataro. 1984. "Application of Play-Oneiric Tests in Basic Motivational Research and Communication Studies." In *Proceedings*, 649–68. Rome, Italy: ESOMAR Congress, September.
Gardner, B. 1959. "The ABC's of Motivation Research." *Business Topics*, Summer, 35–41.
Gottlieb, M. J. 1985. "Code Segmentation by Personality Types." In *Advancing of Marketing Efficiency*, ed. L. H. Stockman, Chicago: American Marketing Association. 148–58.
Green, P. E., and F. J. Carmone. 1970. *Multidimensional Scaling and Related Techniques*. Boston: Allyn and Bacon.
Gustafson, P. 1958. "You Can Gauge Customers' Wants." *Nation's Business*, April.
Haire, M. 1950. "Projective Techniques in Marketing Research." *Journal of Marketing* 14 (April): 649–56.

Hawkins, Del I., Roger J. Best, and Kenneth A. Coney. 1989. *Consumer Behavior—Implications for Marketing Strategy*. Homewood, IL: BPI-Irwin.

Heylen, J. P. 1984a. "Libido as the Mainspring of Consumer Behavior." In *New Horizons in Marketing*. Stichtin Marketing vzw, 47–59.

———. 1984b. "Towards an Implicit Psychoanalytic Model ('Libido Model') of Consumer Behavior." In *Proceedings*. Copenhagen, Denmark: EMAC/ESOMAR Symposium on Methodological Advances in Marketing Research Theory and Practice, 177–189.

Kendall, M. G. 1968. *A Course in Multivariate Analysis*. London: Charles Griffin.

———. 1975. *Multivariate Analysis*. New York: Hafner Press.

Key, W. B. 1973. *Subliminal Seduction: Ad Media's Manipulation of a Not So Innocent America*. Englewood Cliffs, NJ: Prentice-Hall.

Klein, M. 1983. *Discover Your Real Self*. London: Hutchinson.

Krief, Y. 1984. "A Communication Audit: A Re-defining of the Strategic Study." In *Proceedings*, 561–86. Rome, Italy: ESOMAR Congress.

Kotler, Philip. 1994. *Marketing Management*. Englewood Cliffs, N.J.

Packard, V. O. 1957. *The Hidden Persuaders*. New York: David McKay.

Rothwell, N. D. 1955. "Motivational Research Reinstated." *Journal of Marketing* 19 (October): 150–54.

Samli, A. Coskun, and William C. Wilkinson. 1987. "Demise and Revival of Motivation Research: Recent Lesson from Europe." J. M. Hawes and G. B. Glisan (eds.) *Development in Markeing Science*, Vol. 10. Miami: Academy of Marketing Science, 464–469.

Sampson, P. 1985. "Qualitative Research in Europe: The State of the Art and Art of the State." In *Broadening the Uses of Research*, Proceedings of the 38th ESOMAR Congress, 67–99. Wiesbaden, Germany.

Samuels, J. 1984. "The Impact of the Recession on Professionalism in Market Research in the UK, 1978–1983." In *Proceedings*, 49–72. Rome, Italy: ESOMAR Congress.

Schiffman, L. G., and L. L. Kanuk. 1992. *Consumer Behavior*. Englewood Cliffs, NJ: Prentice-Hall.

Schlackman, W. 1984. "A Discussion of the Use of Sensitivity Panels in Market Research." *Journal of the Market Research Society* 26(3) (July): 191–208.

Scriven, L. E. 1958. "Rationality and Irrationality in Motivation Research." In *Motivation and Marketing Behavior*, ed. R. Ferber and H. G. Wales, Homewood, IL: Richard D. Irwin. 69–70.

Wicken, A. J. 1977. "How Different Is Qualitative Research?" Qualitative Research Supplement to the Market Research Society Newsletter, 132 (November).

10

Managing Marketing Research

INTRODUCTION

The marketing decision maker needs information to be presented in a certain format with specific details and at a specified time and place. Thus, the management of the marketing research activity is critical for the marketing decision maker, who must ensure sure that information (and not just data) will be made available whenever and wherever necessary to facilitate marketing decisions. As presented in Exhibit 10–1, there is always a gap between what the decision maker needs and what the research offers. Although this exhibit is written in a lighthearted manner, those who are involved in research and decision making would acknowledge that the exhibit in essence is not funny because it is too realistic. Good management of the research activity is likely to close the information gap (depicted in Exhibit 10–1). One of the key questions here, of course, is to decide just who is responsible for the management of research. From the marketing decision maker's perspective, regardless of who is managing certain bottom-line activities, they need to be performed so that marketing decisions can be made adequately, effectively, and on time. This chapter explores the function of marketing research management, particularly from the marketing decision makers' perspective. Many of the ideas in this chapter are adopted from Myers and Samli (1969).

INFORMATION NEEDS OF THE DECISION MAKER

Exhibit 10–1 identifies the decision maker's information needs. No matter who is responsible for managing marketing research, in the final analysis, it must fulfill the seven specific needs of the decision maker.

Decision-maker's Needs	Research Offering
• Simplicity (is it yes or no)	Complexity (the response indicates a conditional maybe)
• Practicality (is there a market demand)	Abstractness (consumers indeed indicate a favorable attitude)
• Immediacy (can we enter the market now)	Future useability (it is quite likely that in a year we could)
• Certainty (it is or isn't it)	Probability (maybe)
• Clarity (are these data any good)	Provisionality (if you assume that . . . it is good)
• Continuity (are these data comparable to the previous set)	Disjointedness (please read our methodological changes with care)
• Reliability (are these data reliable)	Conditionality (you must understand that the data have certain shortcomings)

Exhibit 10–1 The Information Gap in Marketing Research

The Seven Specific Needs

Simplicity. Information provided by the research activity must be simple enough to encourage decisiveness. If the decisions are going to improve the firm's well-being in the marketplace, they must be made accurately in order to reduce risk and quickly so that market opportunities will not be lost.

Practicability. Information generated by marketing research must be practical enough that a clear-cut decision area can be identified. Information must indicate if the marketing plan, for instance, is actionable.

Immediacy. The particular information at the disposal of the decision maker must be such that the actions that will follow can be implemented immediately. This means, first, that information generated by research cannot be outdated, and second, that it must facilitate immediate action.

Certainty. If the information does not reduce the risk factor, it is not important enough. Therefore, the marketing decision maker must receive information that is as accurate and factual as possible. Certainly, research activity needs to be substantial enough to generate this type of information.

Clarity. Management should know that the information at its disposal is good and, even more important, it must understand exactly the message behind the information. A lack of communication between the management and research groups, regardless of who is at fault, can be disastrous. Every attempt must be made to provide management with good information that will be clearly comprehended.

Continuity. Although the research staff may have reason to change the data (and even to improve it) unless the management is cognizant of these changes, the benefits will most likely be lost. Marketing decision makers not only must understand the nature of the data but also must be made aware of trends by having continuity in the data. Hence, if the research specialists improve the data or make some changes in the information that is generated, they must adjust the previous data in favor of continuity.

Reliability. If the data are unreliable because the percentage of random errors is high, the decision maker cannot rely on it for critical marketing decisions. A lack of reliability basically implies that similar results may not be obtained by repeating the research process.

Marketing research activity must be organized to provide the decision maker's needs, as specified in Exhibit 10–1. As a staff function, marketing research does not need to be connected to the line organization directly. However, if it is not close to the marketing decision maker, its reason for existence needs to be questioned.

After having discussed the information gap between the researcher and the marketing decision maker, it is necessary to look further into the management of the research process. Here, there are critical differences between the research user and the director of research. Exhibit 10–2 highlights the key areas of discrepancy between the two parties.

PERCEPTION OF GAPS BETWEEN RESEARCH DIRECTOR AND THE RESEARCH USER

Krum, Rau, and Keiser (1987–1988) analyzed how researchers and users of research in Fortune 500 manufacturing firms perceive the importance of market research at each phase of the marketing research process. They explored many aspects of the research process and the degree of congruence between the research director and the research user. Exhibit 10–2 illustrates only those key areas where incongruence between the two parties was predominant. In managing research, these must be the highest-priority areas for resolution if marketing research is to be maximally supportive of the firm's strategic plans and their implementation.

	Research Director	Research User
The researcher should be involved in marketing strategy of the firm.	+	+ *
Researcher should restrict his activities and offer advice only when asked.	+	+ *
Researcher must determine ongoing information needs and have the information available when needed.	+ *	÷
Researcher must help the management define the problems to be studied.	+ *	+
Researcher must have the final say concerning the methodology.	+ *	+
The researcher should be able to translate marketing research results into courses of action for management to follow.	+ *	+

+ Agreement that the decision should be made by that person.

+ * Significantly higher response by that group.

Exhibit 10–2 Decision Gap between Researchers and Research Users in Marketing Research. *Source:* Adopted and revised from Krum, Rau, and Keiser (1987–1988).

There are seven critical conflict areas in the perception of the role of marketing research depicted in Exhibit 10–2. The first key area of disagreement is in the area of whether the researcher should be involved in marketing strategy development for the firm. Research directors did not agree with this stance nearly as frequently as research users. Perhaps this and other aspects of Exhibit 10–2 indicate some confusion between staff and line functions. The researcher should be involved in strategic planning and implementation only to the extent that he or she provides information as to what the research objectives should be and what kind of data should be gathered.

The second discrepancy is in the area of whether researchers should restrict their activities and offer advice only when asked. More research users opted for this alternative. However, this condition can be dangerous if the marketing decision maker is not sophisticated enough to ask critical questions and receive help when needed.

The third conflict area is related to the researchers' need to determining ongoing information requirements and to have this information available when needed. Surprisingly, research directors are more in agreement with this position than research users. Perhaps, the research users here may have perceived the situation as losing power. Certainly, determining information needs has to be a joint activity of both groups; however, gathering data methodically and generating the necessary information regularly can be extremely important for a firm's competitive advantage. If the necessary information is readily available, the firm's marketing decisions are most likely to be swift, timely, and effective.

As seen in Exhibit 10–2, the fourth conflict raises the question of whether the researcher should help management define the problems to be studied. Research directors agreed with the affirmative significantly more than the research users. Defining the problem must be a two-stage activity. Marketing decision makers (research users) must identify the management problem areas, while the second stage should be the interpretation of the management's problems into research needs. Thus, once again, it is necessary for both parties to collaborate fully.

Regarding whether the researcher must have the final say concerning the research methodology, research directors were overwhelmingly in agreement. Marketing management should go along with this position. It is the research specialist's responsibility to determine how the data are best obtained and what are the most appropriate data for the problem at hand.

Whether the researcher should be able to translate marketing research results into courses of action for management to follow is the sixth conflict area. Whereas research directors agreed with this position, a substantially smaller number of research users responded in the affirmative. Researchers must have the responsibility to interpret the data, but it is the research user who subsequently has the responsibility to develop the courses of action to be followed.

Finally, the last conflict area depicted by Exhibit 10–2 is related to the persuasiveness of the researcher in making the management accept research findings. Again, whereas the research director's response was a strong affirmative, the user's response was one of nominal agreement. The value of research findings is in their applicability and usability in the decision-making process. If the researcher develops too much author's pride and becomes overly involved in the research process and results, then the true value of research will be diminished. Researchers must know that the company's best interest is their best interest as well. Hence, overselling research findings should not be the goal. Instead, the need to generate the most vital information for the management's immediate use must always be kept in mind by both parties.

Thus far, information needs and perception gaps have been discussed. One unrelated, but absolutely essential, decision area in research management is the research budget. It must be decided at the beginning just how much needs to be spent on research so that the firm can gain or enhance its competitive advantage.

HOW MUCH FOR RESEARCH

When facing a decision, the marketing manager must answer two questions: (1) whether there should be marketing research to bear on this decision and (2) what should be the scope of this project (i.e., size and accuracy)? Thus, in order to exercise proper management and control, it is necessary, first of all, to establish the economic limits of marketing research. Establishing the economic limits of marketing research is dependent on the *value of information obtained*. If the net advantage of marketing research does not exceed the cost of undertaking such research, then this information is not worthwhile. This section presents five separate techniques that are used to determine the value of information. They are based on Myers' and Samli's (1969) earlier work.

SIMPLE SAVINGS METHOD

This is the simplest form of attempting to estimate the value of research. It is based on an assumption that management can reasonably estimate the cost of making a wrong decision. This method is illustrated in Exhibit 10–3 for a decision that would cost the company $400,000 if made improperly.

If the cost of a wrong decision is estimated at $400,000, the flip of a coin will result in a 50 percent chance of making a right decision; hence, the expected cost of the decision is $200,000. This implies that such decisions in the long run will be wrong half the time. If some information is known, the chances of a correct decision are increased to 60 percent. The use of marketing research is expected to further increase

	Chance of correct decision	Estimated cost of mistake
Making decision by flipping coin	50-50	$200,000
Using known facts in decision (no research)	60-40	160,000
Using additional research information	75-25	100,000
Value of research: $160,000-$100,000 = $60,000		

Exhibit 10–3 Estimated Savings

the chances of making the right decision to 75 percent. In this case, the value of research is, at most, $60,000.

RETURN ON INVESTMENT

This method considers research as an investment, and its worth is calculated after determining the value of its findings. For example, assume that Oscar Mayer Co. reviewed its major marketing research projects during the previous fiscal year. Assume further that in only 30 percent of the decisions was the research information the deciding factor; in other words, in 70 percent of the instances, when managerial decisions were made, the correct decision could have been made without marketing research. The following formula is then used to determine the value of research:

$$\frac{\text{Worth of findings} \times 0.30}{\text{Annual marketing research budget}} = \text{Return on investment}$$

Thus, if the annual research budget is $350,000 and the total information provided is judged to have been worth $2,333,300, the return on investment, by using this formula, is estimated to be approximately 200%. This method enables the company to make an objective estimate of the contribution of marketing research to corporate profitability.

PRESENT VALUE METHOD

This third technique also treats research expenditures as investments. It is based on the computed expected return of an investment. This is done by discounting the incremental cash benefits expected over the lifetime of the investment by the marginal cost of capital:

$$PV = (R_0 - C_0) + \overset{\text{First Year}}{\frac{(R_1 - C_1)}{(1+K)^2}} + \overset{\text{Second Year}}{\frac{(R_2 - C_2)}{(1+K)^n}} + \overset{\text{Final Year}}{\frac{(R_n - C_n)}{1+K}}$$

where PV = present value of the research expenditures.
$R_0 \ldots R_n$ = annual cash receipts attributable to the investment.
$C_0 \ldots C_n$ = the incremental cash expenditures, and
K = firm's marginal cost of capital.

Just as with the previous techniques, this technique can be applied to a research project as well as the total research activity of the firm, and it offers a more effective approach than the previous techniques.

BAYESIAN ANALYSIS

This, perhaps, is the best way to determine the value of information. The technique sets an upper limit on the amount of money that profitably can be spent on a particular marketing problem before it is decided whether research should take place. This limit is based on the money to be earned or saved by making the correct decision. Bayesian analysis also helps determine which of the several research designs is likely to yield the best return. The unique characteristic of this analysis is that it allows the assignment to special events of numerical subjective probabilities, which are often based on past experience or estimates.

To illustrate this technique, the introduction of a new product is used. Classical approaches provide no basis for establishing the probability of the product's performance in the marketplace unless a nationwide test market is used. Nor do they indicate whether research should take place and, if so, how much should be spent on it. The Bayesian approach, on the other hand, could:

1. Provide probabilities as to the expected success of the product.
2. Determine whether or not marketing research should take place.
3. Establish the upper limit of the sum that can be spent on marketing research.

According to the Bayesian position, management always has some idea of how well a product will do. This is based on past experience (the owners' or competitors'), similarity to other products, evaluation of the new product in respect to its characteristics, promotional plans, and competitive conditions. These feelings can be translated into quantitative terms by asking management to estimate the probabilities of reaching various levels of sales.

Exhibit 10–4 illustrates the Bayesian analysis for a company considering the introduction of a new hand cream for men. Column 1 gives the range of expected sales for the new product. Column 2 shows management's estimate of the probability that the indicated sales volume can be achieved. For example, management estimates a 5 percent probability of having a sales volume of 400,000 units.

For each of the various sales figures, the profit or loss is calculated. This is shown in Column 3. Profits and losses for the various sales range from $400,000 to −$350,000, with a break-even sales point of 1 million units. From this point on, the key concept in the analysis is opportunity loss. This can mean one of the following:

1. Actual amount of money lost from the introduction of the product because sales are below break-even.

			Opportunity Loss		Expected Opportunity Loss	
Unit Sales	Estimated Probability	Profit or Loss	Introduce	Not Introduce	Introduce	Not Introduce
(1)	(2)	(3)	(4)	(5)	(6)	(7)
1,400,000	.10	$400,000	0	400,000	0	$40,000
1,200,000	.25	150,000	0	150,000	0	37,500
1,000,000	.30	0	0	0	0	0
800,000	.20	-100,000	$100,000	0	$20,000	0
600,000	.10	-250,000	225,000	0	22,500	0
400,000	.05	-350,000	350,000	0	17,500	0
					$60,000	$77,500

Exhibit 10–4 Bayesian Analysis for New Product Information

2. Loss of potential profit because of the failure to introduce the product when sales would have been adequate (i.e., greater than 1 million units).

Column 4 shows at what sales volume the introduction of the product will result in opportunity loss. Above the break-even point, the new product is profitable and there is no opportunity loss. Column 5 shows that an opportunity loss will result from the decision not to introduce the product if sales exceed break-even.

Expected opportunity loss for each action, to introduce or not to introduce, is determined by multiplying opportunity losses in Columns 4 and 5 by the probability of these losses, obtained from Column 2. The results are shown in Columns 6 and 7. The sum of opportunity losses for introducing the product is $60,000 and for not introducing it, $77,500. Since the decision to introduce the product creates the lowest expected opportunity loss, the company should choose to do so. If the firm in this case were to obtain research information indicating exactly how many men would buy the new product, it could reduce the expected opportunity loss by, at most, $60,000. Therefore the maximum value of research in this case is $60,000. It would not be reasonable to spend more than this sum on research. Moreover, the assumption remains that research will provide perfect information, which is unrealistic; therefore, the upper limit should be lower than $60,000.

COST-BENEFIT METHOD

Another logical way of calculating the value of marketing research is to determine the amount of the benefits minus the costs. According to

Unit Sales	Research Alternatives		
	R_1	R_2	R_3
1,400,000	.15	.25	.10
1,200,000	.30	.15	.15
1,000,000	.25	.10	.20
800,000	.10	.05	.10
600,000	.05	.10	.15
400,000	.10	.00	.20

Exhibit 10–5 Payoff Matrix for Research Alternatives

this approach, three criteria are used to evaluate information generated by marketing research:

1. Set a cost figure and maximize the benefits to be obtained from that cost.
2. Establish the level of benefits to be obtained and minimize the cost of obtaining them.
3. Maximize the value of benefits.

Applying the cost benefit model to the Bayesian analysis in the previous section, the lowest expected opportunity loss establishes an upper limit on the benefits obtained from research. Added to this, the cost of different research procedures provides a reference point to compare these procedures.

Exhibit 10–5 provides a payoff matrix for three research designs, R_1, R_2, and R_3, (e.g., test market, consumer survey, and motivation research). Entries in the matrix are probabilities that the information provided by the research project will reveal to the decision-maker if each particular sales level will be realized. Thus, there is a 15 percent chance that the first research design (R_1) will indicate that sales will be 1.4 million units. These probabilities are most likely to be established by research personnel who are most familiar with the strengths and weaknesses of these research alternatives.

When these probabilities are weighted by management's estimates of the probabilities of each level of sales (Exhibit 10–4, Column 2), the result is an expected value for the probabilities that each research design will provide perfect information. In this case, as seen in Exhibit 10–6, R_1 has the highest conditional probability of predicting the true state of the marketplace. Method R_1 has the highest conditional probability, and it would be preferred on that basis. However, its relative cost must also be considered. By multiplying the conditional probabilities

$P(P_1/R_1)$ = .10(.15) + .25(.30) + .30(.25) + .20(.10) + .10(.05) + .05(.10) = .195

$P(P_1/R_2)$ = .10(.25) + .25(.15) + .30(.10) + .20(.05) + .10(.10) + .05(.00) = .113

$P(P_1/R_3)$ = .10(.10) + .25(.15) + .30(.20) + .20(.10) + .10(.15) + .05(.10) = .153

Exhibit 10–6 Conditional Probabilities

with the estimated upper limit of research benefits ($60,000), the return to each research design is estimated. By subtracting the estimated cost of each design from its expected return, the net return is calculated. Exhibit 10–7 illustrates that R_2 is the most desirable research approach because it has the best cost-benefit ratio.

MANAGING THE RESEARCH PROCESS

Although it is a staff function, the marketing research process needs to be managed in such a way that it will interact optimally with marketing decision makers. Thus, as marketing research is managed, its interaction with the management of the company, and particularly with marketing decision makers, must be kept in mind as one of the critical factors in this overall activity.

In managing the research process, five specific functions must be considered. Each of these has a different relationship with and varying importance in the eyes of marketing decision makers.

Exhibit 10–8 illustrates how the marketing research process is managed. Six key steps are identified in the exhibit: direct, collect, process, generate, disseminate, and use.

Directing the research process must be a joint activity between the research director and research user in a sense that the management (decision makers or research users) must receive the type of information that is needed. It is maintained here that both parties *jointly* must decide what kind of research must take place and what kind of data and information need to be generated.

	Benefit	Estimated Cost	Benefit Minus Cost
R_1	60,000(.195) = $11,700	16,300	-4,600
R_2	60,000(.113) = $6,780	4,500	2,280
R_3	60,000(.153) = $9,180	8,500	680

Exhibit 10–7 Cost Benefit Analysis for Three Research Alternatives

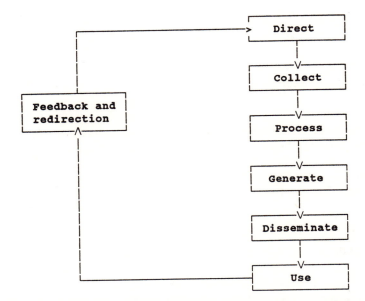

Exhibit 10–8 Management of the Research Process. *Source:* Adapted and revised from Montgomery and Weinberg (1979).

Collecting is almost exclusively a research function. Once the data and information needs have been identified, it is up to the researcher to decide how the data need to be collected, what techniques need to be used, and what are the major sources of data.

Processing the data that are accumulated and generating the necessary information is also exclusively a research function. Certainly, the users of research must understand just what took place in the research process. However, this is strictly for reference purposes. The research group must be free to pursue technical aspects of research. However, the research group must always be cognizant of marketing decision makers' needs, without delay.

Generating information that will facilitate marketing decision making is, after all, the key function of marketing research. Here, the research group must generate a database and an information flow to critical decision-making circles so that all marketing-related decisions can be based on a sound foundation. The flow of information needs to be efficient and swift; however, the nature of the generated information is the most critical concern. Unless the needs of the decision makers are clearly understood, proper databases cannot be developed and these data cannot be converted into the relevant information.

Disseminating the information that is generated is also a prime responsibility of the research group. Here, the information not only must go where it is needed, but also must be in the form that is needed so that it can be used most effectively. A written report, a summary on the computer, or a detailed technical report, both in written form as well as on the computer, are some of the alternatives. It may be that portions of the information will go to different functional decision makers. One of the most important aspects of the information flow is its interactive nature. Marketing decision makers must be able to reach out and receive additional information from the existing databases of information. Here, marketing decision makers may need assistance from the research group, which makes their accessibility very critical. The marketing decision maker must be able to call on the researcher for additional information right there and then.

Finally, using the information is strictly the management's responsibility. Unless the marketing decision maker requests it, the researcher need not specify how the research information should be generated. However, decision makers should always strive to make good use of the talent, knowledge, and availability of the research group. In fact, consulting with the research group before reaching critical decisions makes good sense.

Finally, there is a seventh function that is dwelled on in Exhibit 10–8, which is kept separate because it is related to all six of the first group of functions. This is the feedback function, which is needed for redirecting the research process where redirection is needed. In all stages of the research process, a self-evaluation activity (feedback) must take place. In some circumstances, feedback may mean a repeat effort to generate the database and to extract the necessary information. Otherwise, less-than-adequate information may lead to less-than-optimal marketing decisions. This kind of redirection enhances the total system's effectiveness.

SUMMARY

This chapter deals with the key issue of managing the research process so that it will provide the best support for marketing decision makers. First, the gaps between the decision makers' needs and what the research group offers are discussed. Seven specific gaps are identified: simplicity, practicability, immediacy, certainty, clarity, continuity, and reliability.

Another set of gaps is related to marketing research design. Here also, seven key areas of disagreement are identified. Marketing research users and research directors have different opinions as to how the research should be conducted. Here, the critical factor is the agreement by both parties. These gaps will minimize the effectiveness of marketing research.

One of the most important areas of research management is to identify the value of research in terms of dollars and cents. Five separate techniques are presented in this chapter, all of which can be used to determine the size of the research budget: simple savings, return on investment, present value, Bayesian analysis, and cost-benefit analysis.

Finally, in actual management of the research process, six key functions are identified: direct, collect, process, generate, disseminate, and use. In all six, a feedback and, subsequently, a redirection activity are required.

REFERENCES

Krum, James R., Pradeep A. Rau, and Stephen K. Keiser. 1987–1988. "The Marketing Research Process." *Journal of Advertising Research* (December/January): 9–21.

Montgomery, David B., and Charles B. Weinberg. 1979. "Toward Strategic Intelligence Systems." *Journal of Marketing* (Fall): 41–49.

Myers, James H., and A. Coskun Samli. 1969. "Management Control of Marketing Research." *Journal of Marketing Research* (August): 267–77.

11

Developing Information from Data

INTRODUCTION

Throughout this book a major point of emphasis has been the distinction between data and information. Using these two interchangeably is a common mistake that may prove to be very costly to a firm. Unless the data are processed and put into a form that will facilitate the decision-making process, they are of little value. Thus, the data need to be transformed into information. As stated in Chapter 1, in recent years there has been much emphasis on gathering data and generating databases (or data banks) without paying enough attention to how the data are processed so that usable information can be generated. This chapter presents some of the major philosophical arguments relating to data processing and, hence, information generation. In addition to this philosophical discussion, a brief description of the data analysis techniques that have been developed during the past three decades or so is presented. Once again, the focus here is providing necessary knowledge for marketing decision makers, who will not be directly involved in the research activity but will play the key role in the decision-making process.

FROM DATA TO INFORMATION

Exhibit 11–1 indicates the basic connection between data and marketing decisions. Data need to be processed before information can be generated. In recent years, because of the sophisticated technology, part of the data-processing activity has become automatic. However, tech-

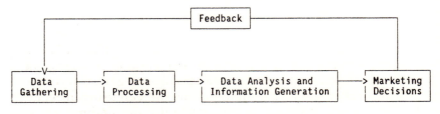

Exhibit 11-1 From Data to Decision Making

nology-controlled data processing, almost by definition, limits the nature and quality of data. The more involved and complex the data are, the more difficult to process them to the best advantage of the user.

The data-processing activity is a five-step approach (Exhibit 11–2). Since the marketing decision-maker must have only a general comprehension of these steps, they are written rather briefly. The reader is referred to any marketing research textbook for some technical details. However, the points emphasized here may not be readily available in a typical marketing research book.

Editing and Coding

Editing. Editing is very critical in generating quality data. The marketing decision maker must know that the data were originally edited.

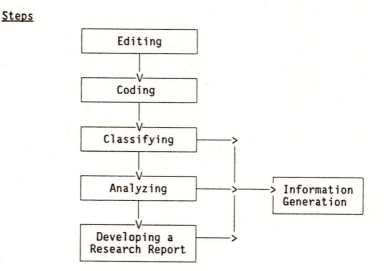

Exhibit 11-2 The Data-Processing Activity

Editing *in the field* makes sure that the data were collected, using the specified procedures, from the intended places, markets, or other participants. Editing *in the office* delves into elimination of inconsistencies in the data, correction of irrelevant or incomplete data, standardization of responses by classifying them into specific categories, and finally, processing of open-ended questions that are difficult to organize. Eliminating erroneous information and validating the findings are also critical activities of office editing.

Coding. Coding is assigning symbols to quantify all the qualitative bits of responses from different groups of people during the course of a survey. A coding system is extremely critical to generate and organize the data before they become information. There are certain features that a good coding system should have: (1) flexibility, (2) ease of implementation, (3) retrievability, (4) efficiency, (5) adequacy, and (6) format.

Flexibility means that the coding system can put together a database that can be used for many different decision areas. In fact, such a feature in a database is essential. Only with the help of such flexibility will the firm's decisions be swift and versatile. The coding system should be easy to apply yet sufficiently profound to facilitate complicated decision areas. The ease of the coding system is likely to accelerate the quality of the data base.

The coding system should provide retrievability. Having the data in the system without the ability to retrieve them makes the whole process an exercise in futility. The coding system must facilitate retrieving the data as needed in any shape and form. A good data retrieval system should allow users to exercise strategic search choices quickly and easily and, hence, to explore the application of the research data to the company's marketing decisions (Bates 1990). Efficiency of the coding system is measured on the basis of whether any part of the data is wasted in the process of coding. All the bits of survey responses must be entered into the database through an efficient coding system.

All databases need to be updated, while some need to be revised and perhaps purged. The coding system must be capable of this in order to be adequate for what it is designed to do. Finally, the coding system must provide for the necessary format. The data should be in the type of format that would facilitate information generation as well as the decision-making processes.

These are basic generalizations about the coding system. They should make good sense to those who use research findings closely and often enough. All six features accelerate the overall quality of the database in such a way that the firm, as a whole, will make better decisions and will enhance its competitive advantage in the marketplace.

Classifying

Classification, in essence, means increasing the homogeneity of heterogeneous data, by grouping them according to a preselected common denominator. In fact, the selection of this common denominator (or common denominators) is very critical for the decision maker. The data must become homogeneous in those critical areas where the decision making has highest priorities. Of course, in recent years, classification and coding may be done simultaneously. Current technology in information systems (IS) provides such a capability. Just what are some of the key preselected common denominators on which the data classification may be based? There are at least six such areas in marketing: (1) temporal, (2) spatial, (3) judgmental, (4) functional, (5) preferential, and (6) demographic and lifestyle.

A *temporal* dimension implies using some time unit in grouping the data. If, for instance, the researcher is interested in the people's attitude towards a retail store, the reaction to a survey of respondents who have lived and shopped in that town for more than, say, five years would be more important than those who lived there less than six months. By the same token, if the town is rapidly growing, the opinion of those who have come to town recently may be extremely important. Their attitudes toward a retail store or total retail facilities may be analyzed in detail so that these facilities can be improved.

Spatiality may take a number of forms. In a field survey, the geographic area where the respondents reside is the first form. In a bank image study, for instance, in order to determine the drawing power of a shopping center, the license plate numbers of the cars parked on the facility might be traced back to where the owners resided. Hence, it would be possible to determine where the major number of shoppers came from. In classifying the survey results, the respondents who reside at a distance of a five-minute drive as opposed to twenty-five-minute drive may indicate significant differences in the attitudes toward the shopping facility. A third form of spatiality is related to location preferences. In a survey of a housing market, knowing where people would like to buy or build a new home is most important in determining the future of the housing market in a particular area.

The *judgmental* dimension is related to subjective values of the respondents and/or the evaluation of the researcher. In a central business district study, survey results were classified according to the response to the question, "How do you like the shopping facilities in the Central Business District?" The precoded answers included, "excellent," "good," "fair," "inadequate," and "poor." Classification of the total data was based on each one of these judgmental responses, which in turn indicated which groups or subgroups were satisfied with the central business district as opposed to those who were not satisfied.

The study indicated that those who were satisfied were living in the closest proximity. They were of a lower socioeconomic category with low education, unskilled labor jobs, high unemployment, and very low income. They owned fewer cars and, therefore, did not complain about the highways and parking facilities. However, the picture was completely reversed when the response of those who were dissatisfied was analyzed. They were members of the higher socioeconomic groups, who lived further away from the central business district and were dissatisfied with the complete shopping facility and its accessibility. Thus, classification of the data on these bases illustrated some of the basic ills of the facility but, more important, some of the cures if these socioeconomic groups were to be attracted as a future developmental objective of the total facility.

The evaluation of the researcher also can play an important role in classification of data. Subjective observation is a case in point. In one study, for instance, a hypothesis was tested that two different department stores that are located close to each other were each drawing their own clientele. One of the stores was a discount department store; the other was a high-status department store. They were located about half a block apart. A team of field observers undertook two tasks.

First, they observed what proportion of the customers of either store visit the other store during the same shopping trip. Second, they subjectively evaluated typical customers by keeping a tally of those coming out of the stores separately. Classification of the answers was based on sex, age, and most important, high, middle, or low socioeconomic categories. In the latter, a substantial degree of subjectivity was exercised. However, they attempted to offset the bias by rotating the observers. The researcher in many different types of research may exercise subjectivity in classifying data in a purposeful manner.

Functional classification implies a key activity on the part of the respondents. In a tourist study, for instance, tourists who considered coming to Michigan and those who actually came to Michigan were analyzed separately to establish specific differences (if any) in these two groups. Similarly, in another study, a tally was kept of those pedestrians who went into a store and purchased something as opposed to the total traffic. Hence, it was possible to determine the ratio of the passengers to potential customers.

The *preferential* dimension indicates the degree of intensity of respondents' preferences. As an attempt to determine a market potential for an ice cream parlor, people in the vicinity may be questioned as to whether they go to ice cream parlors. The classification of the answers on a yes-or-no basis enables the researcher to pursue further to determine what proportion of the positive respondents consumed how much ice cream and, of the negative respondents, what proportion may be persuaded to go to an ice cream parlor in the neighborhood.

Similarly in undertaking a comparative study of different shopping centers, households participating in a survey may be classified according to their shopping center preferences (or any other type of preference). The survey results may be analyzed accordingly in an effort to determine the significant differences and similarities among the different shopping center goers.

The *demographic and lifestyle* classification can be very critical in understanding a firm's target markets. As the total market can be broken into specific age, income, education, and other categories, the lifestyles of the members of these categories may help identify and prioritize the markets that the firm should consider. The behavior patterns and mass media exposure can help develop marketing plans that are quite effective for the specific target markets in mind. The critical point is that there is enough flexibility and good data in the data bank of the firm to be used in making the best possible decisions.

Analyzing

The process of analyzing the data and generating information is, in essence, a diagnosis of the firm's problems (if any) and should lead to a specific solution. It is necessary for the marketing decision makers to understand the types of analysis that are at their disposal. Exhibit 11–3 presents a general description of these options. However, before a discussion of these options is presented, it is necessary to identify univariate, bivariate, and multivariate approaches and the philosophy in employing multivariate techniques.

The research must know when to use univariate, bivariate, or multivariate approaches. Exhibit 11–4 illustrates what the marketing decision maker must understand regarding univariate, bivariate, or multivariate analysis. If we need to know about the average age, income, education, or other characteristic of our customers, averages such as mean, median, and mode will be used. Although, say, the average age of a firm's customers may be important for some aspects of the decision-making process, it may be critical to know the characteristics of the loyal customers. Thus, contrasting loyal customers with less loyal customers may become more critical and the analysis would shift from univariate to bivariate approaches (Exhibit 11–3). However, we may decide that more information is needed regarding our loyal customers. We may contrast them, not only with less loyal customers but, perhaps, with the least loyal customers or with noncustomers (those who do not currently use the firm's products). Here, statistical analysis will

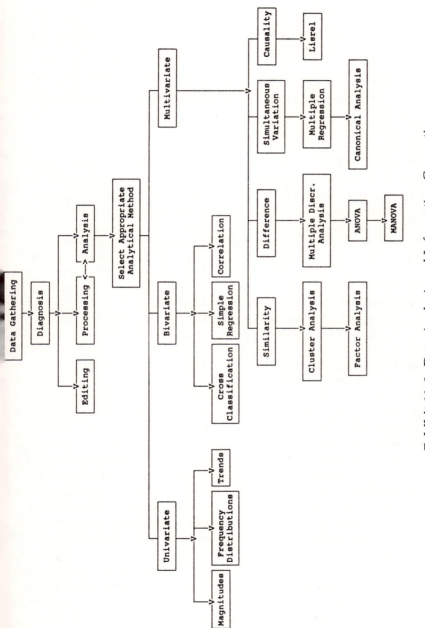

Exhibit 11–3 Data Analysis and Information Generation

Univariate	Bivariate	Multivariate
What is the average income of our customers?	What is the educational background of our loyal and least loyal customers?	What are the purchase behavior characteristics of our loyal customers, less loyal customers, and least loyal customers?

Exhibit 11–4 A Simple Comparison of Univariate, Bivariate, and Multivariate Approaches

move from bivariate to multivariate technique (Exhibit 11–4). There are many statistical techniques used for multivariate analysis to "focus upon, and bring out in bold relief, the structure of simultaneous relationships among three or more phenomena" (Hair et al. 1979, 20).

Magnitudes are single figures. Whether a mean, median, mode, or simply a specific figure, a single magnitude does not reveal much in terms of research findings. When they reveal central tendencies in a group of statistical data, they present some information on the general scope of the data or produce a summary. The arithmetic mean is one of the most widely used magnitudes. It is what is commonly called the average; it measures the point around which the values under study balance. It is utilized in a practical manner in that much marketing data, as in mean sales per month or per store, mean order, mean sales volume per customer, and so forth.

A lesser known concept is the *geometric mean*, which is a more typical average than the arithmetic mean. In order to simplify their computations, geometric means are normally computed through use of logarithms. *Median* and *mode* are two other measures of common tendency of a frequency distribution. The median is the middle item when the data have been arranged according to size. The size of extreme values does not affect the median, while the number of items does. For much asymmetrical marketing data, the median is more representative than the mean. Marketing data often present a skewed distribution. In such cases, the median is smaller than the mean and a better indicator of the middle value.

Finally, the mode is the single value that appears most often in the gathered data. By observing or counting the frequency distribution, the mode can easily be established. Its value is independent of extreme items. In bimodal or multimodal frequency distributions, it is better to look for the modes than to search for other types of common tendency. If, for instance, a new furniture polish put out by Johnson's Wax is reported to be utilized heavily for automobiles as well as for furniture, then it is better to look for modes so that a decision can be made as to whether the product should be marketed as a car polish or a furniture polish.

DISPERSION OF DATA

In an attempt to generate information from the data, although it is important for the marketing researcher to detect common tendencies, it is equally important to measure dispersion. In two separate markets, for instance, while average income is the same, the distribution may be substantially different. Assuming that a better distribution indicates a better market, results regarding the dispersion of income may become a most important measure in determining better markets. There are many methods used to measure dispersion. Two of the most common are the sample variance and the standard deviation. The sample variance measures the distribution of values in the sample around the mean. A greater variance implies a greater dispersion of values from the mean.

The *standard deviation* is another commonly accepted measure of dispersion. It is the square root of the variance. This important concept is extensively utilized in statistical inferences. In sufficiently sizable probability samples, means of samples are normally distributed around the universe mean. Standard deviation measures this distribution.

Trends are a particular longitudinal analysis of one particular variable. Analyzing the past data provides the basis for future estimates. The assumption here is that the pattern in the past behavior will hold true in the future as well.

Although measuring general tendencies or dispersion in one set of marketing data is important, the relationship between these data and some other data may generate more meaningful information that will be of greater value to the marketing decision maker (Exhibit 11–4). The degree of interdependence between sales volume (dependent variable) and advertising expenditures (GNP) (independent variable), or the relationship between gross national product (independent variable) and industry sales (dependent variable), are important bits of information for marketing decisions. Thus bivariate analyses are quite useful. Correlation and regression analyses are the most popular techniques for establishing the degree of association between different variables (Exhibit 11–3).

The degree of linear association between dependent and independent variables can be established by correlation analysis using questions such as these: What is the relationship between the income of consumers and their purchase patterns? How much increase in advertising is needed to attain a 10 percent increase in sales volume? What would the impact be of a 10 percent reduction in prices on the sales volume? What would the expected increase be in the sales volume of the company if the expected increase in the GNP is 6 percent?

Although they are similar techniques, regression analyses indicate the nature of the relationship between the dependent and independent variables while correlation illustrates the extent of this relationship.

MULTIVARIATE ANALYSES

In typical marketing situations, there usually are multitudinous factors interacting between the firm's marketing efforts and the responses of the marketplace (Sheth 1969). It is more realistic to analyze the marketing research data by using techniques that can handle numerous variables simultaneously. For instance, demand for appliances is likely to be a function of prices, promotional activities, and income of the prospective customers, as well as their outlook about the economic conditions and their own economic safety. Naturally, univariate or bivariate techniques cannot handle such a problem as complex as this. However, marketing decision makers need information to prepare a marketing plan for appliances. With the advancement of high powered computers during the past two and a half decades, tremendous progress has taken place in this area. Numerous techniques have been either developed or made applicable to marketing problems.

When there are a number of sets of data to be analyzed, four key approaches may be used: similarity, differences, simultaneous variations, and causality (Exhibit 11–3). Marketing decision makers must be in a position to clearly understand what these four approaches can do, and why. Thus, they can clearly perceive their information needs and understand how to satisfy them.

The Four Key Approaches

Similarity. In analyzing sets of data, one key approach is to analyze them on the basis of their similarities. From a set of data based on a survey taken among the customers of Lazarus in Columbus, Ohio, a major retail establishment, an attempt may be made to find the similarities among the loyal customers and compare them with those of less loyal customers (Exhibit 11–4). For instance, information that loyal customers are younger, better educated, more often married, more professional, earn more money, and are more readily exposed to certain mass media than the other two groups, indicate where the key market lies. By comparing such similarities, the components of marketing plans can be identified by marketing decision makers. With such plans they are capable of satisfying the existing markets and reaching out to "like" markets based on similarities.

Difference. It is quite possible that differences rather than the similarities may be more critical for the firm. Although, for instance, similarities are sought out for identifying target markets, there may be critical differences among consumer groups. Although there are a large variety of similarities between the black and white professional women in their apparel purchase behavior, there are just enough critical differences that an inner city boutique needs to emphasize and cater to perhaps the immediate markets that are most likely composed of black professional women (Samli, Tozier, & Harps 1978).

Simultaneous Variations. The third distinct approach in multivariate analysis is simultaneous variations. Instead of analyzing the data on the basis of similarities or differences, by analyzing the parallels in the variations of different sets of data, valuable information can be generated. Without having any causal explanations, to establish that reducing prices by 10 percent stimulates sales more than increasing advertising expenditures by 10 percent can be extremely important in developing marketing plans. Only multivariate techniques that determine simultaneous variations can generate such information from sales and other expenditure data.

Causality. It is very critical for marketing decision makers to know what causes a given event so that if more of that event is needed, the cause can be augmented. Whereas most of the multivariate techniques do not imply or identify causality, one recently developed technique claims such performance. That technique is LISREL, which is briefly described later on (Exhibit 11–3).

In many cases, these four approaches in multivariate analyses, imply the presence of an analytical philosophy. Certainly, similarity versus differences illustrates an orientation. Emphasizing similarity can be labeled production orientation since like markets can help increase the volume and take advantage of economies of scale. Similarly, concentrating on differences implies sensitivity to market needs and, hence, is perhaps more marketing-oriented. Finally, the decision maker may need more in-depth information relating to dynamic models. The firm may be pursuing an expansion mode, and its marketing plans may require information that is significant in illustrating the firm's activities and their impact on its market performance or other important causalities.

MULTIVARIATE ANALYSIS TECHNIQUES

Cluster Analysis

Cluster analysis is a generic term for all methods related to grouping people or variables (Sheth 1969). Many are based on calculating similarities between persons or variables and grouping them according to their degree of similarity. An individual with scores on m variables is treated as a point on an m-dimensional space; similarly, a variable on which N individuals have scores is treated as a point on an N-dimensional space. The degree of similarity between these two points is calculated by measuring the distance between the two by using one of a series of judgmental rules. If the distance is great, the similarity is negligible. Green, Frank, and Robinson used the distance concept to create clusters of cities that could be considered test markets (Green, Frank & Robinson 1967). In one study of sales trends in small computer sales, for instance, computers were grouped on the basis of their proximity to each other as indicated by their location in different areas of the product space. Cluster 1 lost most of its sales volume, while clusters 2 and 5 made substantial progress. Cluster 1 had over 80 percent of the total sales in 1986; by 1991 this figure had gone down to 10.82 percent of the total. This finding, first of all, indicated that this line of computers had become obsolete. Secondly, findings indicated that clustering in 1991 was not as pronounced as in 1986. This is due to the fact that manufacturers offered a wider variety of products located in different areas of computer product space (Ford 1974). However, it is also important to note that the common product features that are detected in clusters 2 and 5 may indicate the success for the new entrants into this field. New models offered by existing companies or by newly established firms may have to have a minimum of these product features in order to improve their chances of success.

Factor Analysis

Factor analysis is one of the most widely used multivariate techniques in marketing (Sheth 1969). It identifies the underlying factors or forces affecting the relationship between a set of variables (Aaker & Day 1990). According to this technique, original variables indicate mainly superficial aspects of real relationships. By determining the factors that are common to a number of these variables, the real picture can be identified (Sheth 1969). Through this technique we can determine the nature of market segments in terms of similarity of product or brand mix the households purchase, or we can predict private brand purchases for household appliances according to socioeconomic characteristics. Finally, through this technique, a new set of variables can be created for further analyses, which are weighted averages of the original variables. The weights are developed through factor analysis (Massey 1962).

Factor analysis is a method of determining the underlying K variables (factors) from n sets of measures ($K < n$). It is a process of reducing a set of data into a more compact form. A hypothetical illustration might clarify its use. Assume an analysis of six product characteristics. These are measured by different tests. After these tests are administered and scored, correlation coefficients are computed for every test with every other test. It is a matrix that is a rectangular array of numbers. Correlation matrices are always symmetrical (i.e., the lower half of the matrix below the diagonal is exactly the same as the upper half). There are two questions this matrix can help us answer. First, how many underlying unities or factors are behind these test performances? Second, what are these factors? From the nature of the processed data, the first question can be easily answered. There may be two factors. This can be indicated by two separate clusters, I and II. It may be seen that recognition correlates with preference (0.74); recognition with image (0.63); and preference with image (0.59). Thus, recognition, preference, and image are measuring something in common. Similarly, price correlates with style (0.59), price with quality (0.63), and quality with style (0.74). Hence, they are measuring something in common as well. However, they are not measuring the same thing as the first cluster. There are therefore two factors in this matrix. The first factor is related to consumer attitude toward the product. The second is product characteristics as a single factor. This hypothetical case briefly illustrates that in essence there are two key factors: consumer attitude and the product characteristics.

Some Applications in Marketing. Sheth (1969) distinguished five different ways of using factor analysis in marketing.

1. Inference of dimensions that latently order products or brands in terms of consumer preferences. In such cases, the raw data is obtained in the preference ranking or rating of products or brands. After having factor analyzed it, the researcher tries to interpret the relationships or factors once again. In an early study of candy bars, for instance, Stoetel (1960) identified three factors. These were sweetness, price, and regional popularity factors. The same approach has been used for numerous products and services (Sheth 1969).
2. Pattern or structural analysis of a set of attributes. We can obtain structure or pattern among a set of variables by using factor analysis. Obtaining patterns of supermarket choice, propensity to

buy, brand choice (Sheth 1969), or discount store image (Aaker & Day 1990), are some of the areas of application in this particular manner.

3. Separation and analysis of distinct groups or clusters of variables or individuals that exist in the sample. Using factor analysis in order to cluster variables or individuals was displayed in a number of studies (Sheth 1969).

4. Identification of key variables for further analysis from a large set of variables. Twedt (1952), for instance, identified three key variables after having factor-analyzed some nineteen predictor variables and a criterion variable. These three variables yielded a high multiple correlation coefficient.

5. Summarization of correlated variables into a set of explanatory factor variables to remove collinearity in regression or discrimination analysis. Through factor analysis large sets of data can be reduced to a much smaller and manageable set (Sheth 1969; Day & Aaker 1990). It also removes collinearity, if any, in the original variables and, as such, it facilitates studies such as explaining variability in brand loyalty for a variety of products.

Multiple Discriminant Analysis

In order to describe this technique, assume two groups: residents and out-of-towners. Further, assume that a survey was taken involving these two groups. The respondents were questioned about the characteristics of downtown shopping facilities. In order to compute linear discriminant function, its coefficients must first be computed.

$$D = aX_1 + bX_2 + cX_3 + dX_4$$

where D denotes the disciminant function; a, b, c, and d are the coefficients; and X_1, X_2, X_3, and X_4 indicate the measures of the respondents' attitudes towards four specific features of the downtown retail facilities (i.e., quality of goods, selection, prices, and ease of shopping). The discriminant function for the residents was calculated to be $D_1 = 0.5806$ as opposed to that of nonresidents, $D_2 = 0.2666$. The results indicated that, first, there is a significant difference between the attitudes of residents and nonresidents. The residents have a more positive attitude towards the downtown retail facilities. Even more importantly, the relative weight of prices, for instance, appeared to be lower than the others. The discriminating power of prices was low as a separate entity as well as in conjunction with other three factors. Obviously, such a find can provide a basis for a strategy decision relating to the drawing power of the downtown shopping facilities. If the merchants of the downtown shopping facilities have been emphasizing prices as a distinguishing strength of their retail facility, they have wasted effort in emphasizing an attribute that customers do not discriminate.

It must be added that there are various techniques of computing discriminant functions. Analyses can be carried out for more than two groups. Even though manually this is a highly involved procedure, with modern computers this is done very easily.

An interesting classical study (Frank, Massy, & Morrison 1964) employing multiple discriminant analysis was based on the data gathered on Folgers' introduction of regular coffee in the Chicago metropolitan area in 1959. The following question was considered: To what extent do we, the households that adopted Folgers, systematically differ from those that did not, in terms of either our socioeconomic or purchasing characteristics before the time of introduction?

Coefficients were computed for both six and twenty variables. A number of interesting hypotheses can be formulated on the basis of the impact of socioeconomic and purchase characteristics on the probability to adopt Folgers. A wife's employment status appears to be the most important socioeconomic characteristic. Working wives have a lower probability of adopting Folgers (perhaps because they are less aware of innovations?).

On the other hand, income, education, and occupation are not related to the adoption process. (The latter were deleted from the function because of their low degree of significance.) All in all, social class has little if any effect on innovative behavior.

In analyzing the purchasing characteristics, the level of purchases of regular coffee and groceries play no role in whether or not households will adopt Folgers. The relative importance of beverages, on the other hand, in the household budget is positively associated with the adoption probability.

Brand loyalty also appears to be related to adoptive behavior. Households that tend to concentrate a high proportion of their purchases on their favorite brand have a lower probability of adopting a new entrant than those that are less loyal (Frank, Massy, & Morrison 1964).

Studies can easily use discriminant analysis primarily for prediction. For instance, by distinguishing loyal and switching Ford and Chevrolet buyers, it is possible to predict the purchases. Similarly, it is possible to discriminate between those who would send for a program guide to a radio station and those who would not.

ANOVA

Analysis of variance (ANOVA) is concerned with differences between groups or differences in the outcomes of experimental treatments. It primarily deals with the relationship between a single metric dependent variable and a single, nonmetric, independent variable. The independent variable can be at two or more treatment levels. On the basis of ANOVA, key population differences can be estimated from the sample groups. Comparisons of these sample groups for the marketing decision maker may indicate real differences in different market segments (Hair, Anderson, Tatham, & Grablowsky 1979).

MANOVA

Multivariate analysis of variance (MANOVA) is merely an extension of ANOVA. It is a statistical technique that can be used to study the effect of multiple independent variables measured all at the same time. It is used when the indepenent variables are nonmetric. It mainly deals with the real differences among the group (or market segment) mean vectors.

Multiple Regression

Unlike simple correlation or regression, multiple regression is a measure of association between more than one independent variable and a dependent variable. The business of a realtor, for instance, may be dependent on construction contracts awarded, availability of credit, increase in the adult population, disposable income, and real estate prices. A multiple correlation in this case would indicate the importance of all of these factors on the real estate business by showing the goodness of the fit. If there is more than one independent variable, then the function is denoted by:

$$Y = f(X_1, X_2, \ldots X_n)$$

where Y is the dependent variable and is a function of multiple variables that are denoted by $X_1, X_2 \ldots X_n$. Such multiple regressions are very effective in determining the joint impact of a series of independent variables. The use of regression analysis has increased considerably in recent years due to advances in computer technology.

Marketing decision makers must be familiar with scatter diagrams of, for instance, sales volume of a firm and the population of, say, sixteen market areas as the topic for investigation. The best line through the points can be fitted by the regression formula. The closeness of this fit can be determined by the coefficient of determination. The extent to which the regression line explains the variance in the data is measured by the coefficient of determination. As long as all the points in the scatter data are not on the line, this coefficient will be less than +1.0. The square root of the coefficient of determination is called the correlation coefficient and measures the degree of association among variables without determining how much of the total phenomenon can be explained by the independent variables in question.

A partial correlation coefficient measures the degree of association between one independent variable and a dependent variable while all other independent variables are kept constant. In the realtor example above, it is possible to determine the relative association of each of the independent variables with the realtor's sales volume while holding the other variables constant. The mechanics of simple and multiple correlations are explained in any standard statistics book.

Correlation Versus Causation

The correlation coefficient does not necessarily indicate causation. It only measures covariation. A high correlation coefficient may be obtained in any one of the following conditions:

1. A variation in either variable may be caused, directly or indirectly, by a variation in the other.
2. Co-variation of the two variables may be due to a common cause or causes offsetting each variable in the same way or in opposite ways.
3. The causal relationship between the two variables may be due to a result of interdependent relationships.
4. The correlation may be due to chance.

Thus it can be seen that even if there is a causal relationship, the direction of this causation (i.e., determining the dependent and independent variables) cannot be accomplished by correlation analyses only. The researcher and the decision maker must exercise caution in using correlation analyses.

Canonical Analyses

Simple and multiple correlation techniques lend themselves to determining the degree of linear covariation between a single dependent variable and one or more independent variables. Multiple discriminant and factor analyses facilitate comparison by emphasizing similarities or differences among the elements of groups. One common situation, which often occurs in marketing and has not been treated properly thus far, is the covariations between a set of dependent and a set of independent variables, or canonical analysis (Green, Halbert, & Robinson 1966).

Often a marketing phenomenon such as salesmanship can be analyzed by looking at the interaction among many dependent and many independent variables. A salesperson's performance, for instance, is indicated by a set of dependent variables such as sales per month or year, number of sales lost, number of complaints, volume of returns of merchandise sold by the salespersons, and different scores of evaluation based on observation of the supervisors. These variables may be very closely correlated with such independent variables as past experience, intelligence, education, the nature of the training program, the nature of supervision, the incentive system, and the method of compensation:

$$Y_1, Y_2, Y_3, ; ; ; = f(X_1, X_2, X_3, X_4, \ldots)$$

That is, multiple dependent variables are a function of a number of independent variables. Canonical analysis is particularly appropriate when interest is in the overall relation of the *predictor* and the *criterion* variables (Sheth 1969).

LISREL

Instead of determining the degree of association or dissociation, in recent years LISREL has been developed to establish causality among various variables. Based on a very elaborate modeling activity, LISREL uses a maximum-likelihood procedure to identify causal relationships (Bagozzi 1980; Lilien, Kotler, & Moorthej 1992).

DEVELOPING INFORMATION SYSTEMS

At the risk of being somewhat repetitious, this chapter needs to reemphasize the practical aspects of generating information from data. In the literature, this is referred to as building an intelligence system or an information system (Fuld 1992; Daniel 1992; Burrows 1994). Here the critical point is, first, acquiring good data; second, generating information from these data; and, third, proper use of this information, as illustrated in Exhibit 11–5.

In Chapter 10, a discussion is presented regarding managing a database. This chapter emphasizes the process of analyzing the data and generating information. It has been stated that over 3,000 businesses have developed and are using databases (Daniel 1992). In addition to generating information by processing the data according to the corporate needs and managing marketing research activity properly (Chapter 10), it is necessary to consider the essentials of developing an information system (or an intelligence system). Six basic principles are posited in this context

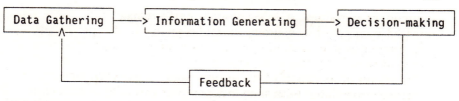

Exhibit 11–5 Generating and Using Information

BASIC PRINCIPLES OF INFORMATION SYSTEMS

Fuld (1992) posited that there are six key principles in developing an information system: (1) coordination, (2) computerization, (3) using internal data, (4) emphasizing long-term benefits, (5) using intelligence-specific software, and (6) generating a critical mass of information.

Coordination

As mentioned in Chapter 4, internal and external data must be brought into one database. Similarly, there are many internal and external data sources. They all need to be coordinated. Finally, if information is generated in different departments or parts of the firm, this information must be incorporated into the total information system. The system must have a commonly shared information pool.

Computerization

Fuld (1992) maintained that as increasing numbers of computer-based intelligence systems are being used, managers must be in a position to decide the characteristics of the system that will serve them best. This may go as far as assessing which hardware and software will be used to generate and deliver information in the most effective and efficient way.

Using Internal Data

Fuld (1992) felt very strongly about the need to rely on internal data, maintaining that such a reliance will generate more timely and accurate information. Relying on public documents too heavily, he maintained, generalizes the system and makes it too broad to be useful for corporate strategy. However, throughout this book it is emphasized that external data must come also through marketing research as it is distinguished from internal accounting and other related data. Thus, internal information must be supplemented, not only external *secondary data* that are already published and available, but also *primary data* generated by the firm's marketing research efforts. A desirable balance is critical between internal and external data (Kavan, Samli, & Frohlich 1993).

Emphasizing Long-Term Benefits

Fuld (1992) maintained that emphasizing long-term benefits of the information system is a catch-22 for managers and stated that effective databases evolve over several years, presenting a problem for the manager who needs to show short-term results. Thus, there must be an understanding regarding short-run and long-run priorities and, particularly, making sure that these two sets of orientations are not working against each other.

Using Intelligence-Specific Software

Information generation, by definition, is based on internally designed database-management software. Similarly information already generated might be made accessible by such computer programs. However, the decision maker's understanding and judgment are very critical here. Once again, the computer is only part of a support system and cannot do what managers need. Therefore, the decision maker must learn how the information is generated, managed, and used (Exhibit 11–5).

Generating a Critical Mass

A successful system must supply timely, accurate, and usable information to its users. Therefore, the system needs constant incoming external and internal data, an improved information process of generation, better information management, and finally, better ways of using the information. This whole system is based on a critical mass of data inflow that must be kept operational at all times.

SUMMARY

The two key issues that are brought out by this book are generating information from data and using this information. These two are identified as information gap and learning gap. This chapter addresses the information gap, and throughout this chapter specific steps for generating information from data are discussed. In addition to editing, coding, and processing, the emphasis is placed on univariate, bivariate, and multivariate analyses. Of these, multivariate analyses in recent years have become more important because of the recognition that there are many identifiable forces in the marketplace that need to be identified and analyzed so that better marketing decisions can be made based on a knowledge of the interaction among these forces and the firm.

In analyzing multiple variables, the marketing decision maker must realize that these variables can be analyzed on the basis of similarities, differences, simultaneous variations, or causality. There are many different techniques that can be used for these analyses. The chapter identifies and briefly describes some key techniques that are used in the areas of similarities, differences, simultaneous variations, and causation.

REFERENCES

Aaker, David A., and George S. Day. 1990. *Marketing Research*. New York: John Wiley and Sons.

Bagozzi, Richard P. 1980. *Causal Models in Marketing*. New York: John Wiley and Sons.

Bates, Marcia J. 1990. "Where Should the Person Stop and the Information Search Interface Start." *Information Processing and Management* 26(5): 575–91.

Burrows, Brian. 1994. "The Power of Information: Developing the knowledge-based organizations." *Long Range Planning,* February: 142–53.

Daniel, Lynn A. 1992. "Overcome the Barriers to Superior Customer Service." *The Journal of Business Strategy* (January/February): 18–24.

Ford, Gary T. 1974. "A Multivariate Investigation of Market Research." In *1974 Combined Proceedings* edited by Ronald C. Curhan, 177–81. Chicago: American Marketing Association.

Frank, R. E., W. F. Massy, and D. G. Morrison. 1964. "The Determinants of Innovative Behavior with Respect to a Branded Frequently Purchased Food Product." In *Reflections on Progress in Marketing*, ed. L. G. Smith, 312–23. Chicago: American Marketing Association.

Fuld, Leonard M. 1992. "Achieving Total Quality through Intelligence." *Long Range Planning,* February, 109–15.

Green, P. E., M. H. Halbert, and P. J. Robinson. 1966. "Canonical Analysis: An Exposition and Illustrative Application." *Journal of Marketing Research* (February): 26–35.

Green, Paul E., R. E. Frank, and P. J. Robinson. 1967. "Cluster Analysis in Test Market Selection." *Management Science* (April): 387–400.

Hair, Joseph F., Jr., Ralph E. Anderson, Ronald L. Tatham, and Bernie J. Grablowsky. 1979. *Multivariate Data Analysis*. Tulsa, OK: Petroleum Publishing Co.

Kavan, C. Bruce, Cheryl J. Frohlich, and A. Coskun Samli. 1994. "Developing a Balanced Information System." *Journal of Services Marketing.* 8(1): 4–13.

Lilien, Gary L., Philip Kotler, and K. Sridhar Moorthej. 1992. *Marketing Models.* Englewood Cliffs, NJ: Prentice-Hall.

Massey, W. F. 1962. "Television Ownership in 1950: Results of a Factor Analytic Study." In *Quantitative Techniques in Marketing Analysis,* ed. R. E. Frank, A. A. Kuehn, and W. F. Massey, 440–60. Homewood, IL: Richard D. Irwin.

Samli, A. Coskun, Enid Tozier, and Yvett Harps. 1978. "Social Class Differences in the Apparel Purchase Behavior of Single, Professional Black Women." *Journal of the Academy of Marketing Science* (Spring): 25–38.

12

Developing Information-Based Marketing Plans

INTRODUCTION

Thus far our discussion has revolved around the development and management of the information system. The system receives its value from the way it facilitates marketing decision making. To the extent that it provides the most appropriate data leading to optimizing the firm's market position and fulfilling its goals, the information system can be considered successful. This chapter illustrates just how the firm's information system can be used to make marketing decisions. In order to accomplish this goal, the chapter systematically analyzes a natural progression in the decision-making process and connects each step in this progression to the information system to identify the effective usage patterns of information in the process.

PREMARKETING STRATEGY DECISIONS

Exhibit 12–1 identifies a five step decision sequence. The key concepts are (1) opportunities, (2) threats, (3) strengths, (4) weaknesses, and (5) priorities.

Opportunities

Determining market opportunities can be analyzed on the basis of the present or the future. Determining current market opportunities is *market potential analysis*. Determining future market opportunities is *forecasting*.

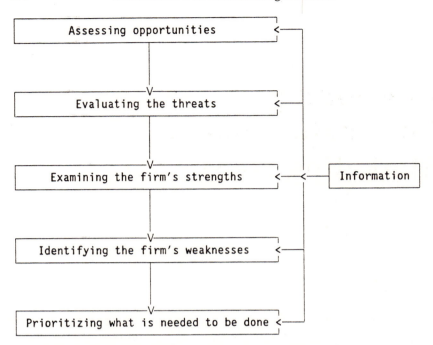

Exhibit 12–1 Premarketing Strategy Decision Sequence

There are many techniques that can be used to determine market opportunities. These techniques can be grouped into three categories: (1) analyzing the sales volume, (2) single factor analysis, (3) multiple factor technique.

Analyzing the sales volume would roughly indicate the current market potentials. Sales volumes are determined by either local sales tax figures or by accumulated data that are available in secondary sources that are already published or readily available in terms of data bases.

Single factor analysis implies determining market potentials based on certain factors. For instance, if the number of households is known and if we know that households, on the average, spend $10,000 per year on food, we can tell what the market potential is for food. Similarly, number of people, number of cars, etc., can be used as a factor to estimate market potentials.

Multiple factor techniques imply using more than one factor to determine market potentials.

Sales and Marketing Management. Buying power index (BPI) is the most widely used example of this technique. Buying power index is

Factors	Blacksburg as a percent of national total		Blacksburg figures adjusted by the weights
Income	.00011 x 5	=	.00055
Retail Sales	.00007 x 3	=	.00021
Population	.00008 x 2	=	.00016
			.00092 ÷ 10 = .000092

[a]Hypothetical figures

Exhibit 12–2 Blacksburg, Virginia, Buying Power Index. *Source:* Samli (1989).

based on three key factors: personal income, which carries the weight of 5; retail sales, which carries the weight of 3; and population, which carries the weight of 2. Exhibit 12–2 presents a hypothetical example that illustrates how BPI works. Blacksburg's share of any national total sales volume is about .00009 percent of the total. By using the national sales figures for, say, groceries, and multiplying that figure by Blacksburg's buying power index (.00009 in this case), we can estimate the amount of groceries likely to be sold in that town. This figure can be further adjusted by using concepts such as the quality index, which implies a ratio between income and population, or index of sales activity, which represents a ratio between population and retail sales (Samli 1989).

As can be seen, multiple factor technique proves more versatility in attempts to determine market potentials. Marketing decision makers must realize that with modern hardware and software it is rather easy to develop their own multiple factor technique by using the variable that they prefer. Once again, the decision maker needs to be close to the data and must understand the information needs. Obviously, in such undertakings, not only the factors may be different, but the weights used can be different. Whereas the weights used in the BPI are somewhat arbitrary, the weights used in a more customized BPI can be more scientific by using partial regression coefficients generated by a multiple regression procedure. There may be other techniques to determine market potentials. Again, the marketing decision maker must know the needs and the alternatives.

Although it is important to know existing market potentials, the nature and scope of these potentials in the near and far future, are vital for future decisions in marketing. Thus, forecasting is extremely important for the marketing decision maker. Most logical approaches to market forecasting are based on three assumptions:

1. Economic magnitudes such as income, prices, production levels are bound together in a system that has considerable stability over time.
2. Future changes in these magnitudes will result, to a substantial extent, from causes operating currently, and they may be deduced from presently observable symptoms.
3. The nature of current symptoms or events, and their probable future consequences, may be discovered by studying past experiences.

On the basis of these assumptions, there have been many attempts to develop forecasting models (Kotler 1994). Determining future market potentials, in general terms, is quite different than forecasting the firm's market share or sales volume. In this context, there has been a strong tendency to utilize trend analyses. In fact, there has been much technical and statistical progress in developing different trend analyses. They analyze what happened in the past carefully and project onto the future. However, whether they are internal (e.g., unique to the firm) or external (e.g., total market projections), trend analyses assume what happened in the past will repeat itself. This assumption, in very dynamic and indeed turbulent American markets, is difficult to support. Events and changes in American markets are not orderly and are not necessarily part of a detectable pattern. In fact, this is why marketing decision makers must be concerned about their information systems and how they are generated.

Within the framework of market potential analysis and forecasting, opportunities can be analyzed in three different dimensions: *intensive growth*, *integrative growth*, and *diversification growth* (Kotler 1994). All three topics belong in the marketing management area. Suffice it to say, however, that each of these three dimensions requires much market potential and forecasting data and, subsequently, much information. The marketing decision maker, along with the support of marketing research, must be able to identify where the growth and profit opportunities are.

Threats

Marketing decision makers must be in a position to assess threats that may be encroaching on their firms. There must be a way to determine the foreseen and unforeseen threats to the company. Identifying these makes it possible for the marketing decision maker to move in the most feasible pathway for the firm. Threats come in different forms and shapes. It is critical that opportunities be scaled down by assessing threats. Hence, the marketing decision maker must have a good under-

	Type of Data
Actual competition	Number of competitors, their size, total sales
Potential competition	Number of new competitors, their size
Turbulence in the market	Significant disruptions
Economic conditions	Growth of personal income, percent of unemployment
Decline in demand	Industry and company sales, changes in population or households
Change in the lifestyles	New trends threatening your product line
Government standards	New government safety and environmental requirements

Exhibit 12–3 Key Threat Factors

standing of the threats. Exhibit 12–3 illustrates some possible threat factors and the data illustrating the characteristics and intensity of these threats. The factors illustrated in the exhibit need very little discussion. Competition, whether it is actual or potential, needs to be assessed. Many marketing practitioners go after the largest market segments. But they fail to assess the competition that is prevalent in that segment.

Competition can be analyzed at different levels. The most general or broad level is at the *customer need level*. The second level is the *industry competition*. The next specific competitive level is the *product-line competition*. The next most specific competitive level is the *organizational competition* (Jain 1993). A final level of competition can be identified: the *brand level*. Exhibit 12–4 illustrates these five levels of competition and the information needs at each level. The marketing decision maker must

	INFORMATION NEEDS
Consumer need level competition	A specific consumer need
Industry competition	The key industries that are catering to these needs, their relative growth, and their market power
Product line competition	Which products are competing with ours in this area
Organizational competition	The companies that are competing with us in this particular product area--which ones are growing, what is their market position
Brand competition	The particular brands of these companies that are competing head-on with ours--what is the relative position of each, their prioritization, positioning our brands

Exhibit 12–4 Different Levels of Competition

have a full appreciation for these information needs and how to use them properly. Once again, this is the *art* of marketing. What is proposed here cannot be accomplished without the experience and knowledge of how to use the marketing information.

Some markets are more turbulent than others (Samli 1993). Therefore, all things being the same, the market that is less turbulent may be preferred. The more stable the market is, the more desirable it is. This is because more long-term marketing plans can be prepared and more predictable results expected.

Unless the company is targeting certain submarginal or marginal markets, the market may not be desirable if the economic conditions are not up to par. Again, if the firm has options, the market with better economic conditions is more desirable.

If the demand that is directly connected to a firm's products is on the decline, there is little incentive to take advantage of market opportunities and the firm may do better by redirecting its efforts. Changes in lifestyles are somewhat related to declining demand. If the firm's products are related to changing lifestyles that will make the firm's products obsolete, then the market may not be worthwhile to pursue.

Finally, government standards are always changing. If these changing standards are directly to influence the firm's products, it may be wiser to preempt the changing regulations by improving the product beyond the minimum government requirements.

The Firm's Strengths and Weaknesses

All firms have strengths and weaknesses. It is critical for the marketing decision maker to examine and assess the firm's strengths with the specific market opportunities that are being investigated in mind. The firm has a variety of strengths. Although these are unique to each firm, in general the firm's strengths may be in the areas of know-how, finances, research, brands and copyrights, human resources, or corporate image, among many others. The marketing decision maker must be in a position to evaluate these strengths and many others. This is a stage beyond data and information; it is based on experience. This is why marketing is an art as well as science. Here the experienced marketing decision maker would know the most important strengths as well as weaknesses and then decide if the strengths will more than offset the weaknesses. Much of the time, the weaknesses are located in the same general areas the strengths. Again, distinguishing and assessing them is the marketing decision-maker's responsibility. Naturally, in all cases the decision maker needs information as well as experience.

Prioritization

The last step in the premarketing strategy decision sequence is prioritization. This is the step that will provide the guidelines to develop the marketing strategy. At this point the marketing decision maker must be in a position to pinpoint the most promising marketing opportunities and establish their priority order.

At this point, developing a new product for a fast-growing market, developing new markets for certain existing products, and diversifying into a certain area by new partnering arrangements may be the highest priorities. Depending upon the knowledge of the marketing decision maker and support of the information system, the prioritization activity can be made more detailed. This detail will help develop the goals, marketing strategies, and, above all, marketing plans.

MARKETING STRATEGY
AND MANAGEMENT PLAN

Exhibit 12–5 displays this book's primary focus. Developing a marketing strategy and the management plan to implement this strategy successfully are what this whole process aims to accomplish. As seen in the exhibit, all this activity is based on an appropriate information system (IS).

Exhibit 12–5 displays four specific steps: (1) establishing the goals, (2) developing a game plan, (3) constructing a marketing plan, and (4) deciding on the details of the four "Ps." Naturally, different components of the information system cater specifically to each of these four decision areas. It is very difficult to determine just which of the "4Ps" is more critical for the firm and therefore requires more information. However, it can easily be asserted that serious negligence of any of the "4Ps" can be detrimental.

Goals

On the basis of the priorities established, the goals of the firm can be established, revised, or maintained. Certainly, all the information from the premarketing strategy decision sequence needs to be used in establishing these goals. The goals will vary from very general, such as increasing the firm's market share or return to its equity, to becoming number one in the market. In addition to general goals at the corporate level, there may be more specific goals at different corporate levels. Thus, information may be needed for these specific levels.

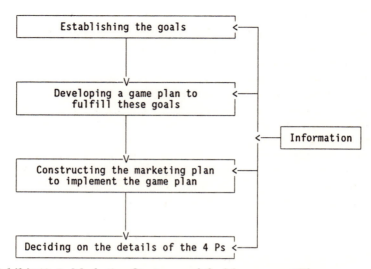

Exhibit 12–5 Marketing Strategy and the Management Plan

The Game Plan and General Marketing Plan

Much has been said and written about strategic plans (Cravens 1994; Jain 1993). Regardless if they are related to entry, penetration, or confrontation (Kotler, Fahey, & Jatusripitak 1985), game plans or strategies are general, action-oriented plans to fulfill the goals.

Assume, for instance, that our company is large with multiple strategic business units. Let us call it Company X. The firm pursues a leadership position in its health and beauty related products. It is making a comeback on its building materials. It is just starting its food processing. Finally, it is maintaining its health food lines. The general game plan has to have multiple components. Based on the information system of the firm, not only are these goals established, how they will be accomplished is also identified.

In this case, Company X must see to it that the health and beauty items are going to be built up, as well as the building materials division. Corporate decision makers will have to decide if both of them are strategic business units (SBUs) and, if so, whether both should be treated equally. Indeed, it is quite likely that the health and beauty items may get more support. As it is specified here, food processing lines may need to be built as well. The health food lines of the company may be simply maintained by holding constant the pertinent activities. It seems the company is not aiming at harvesting or divesting some of its product lines or SBUs.

Product Line	Goals	General Strategic Stance	General Marketing Plans
Health and Beauty Items	Leadership	Build	Heavy research & development Heavy mass promotion Careful emphasis on distribution Some personal selling
Building Materials	Challenger or Follower	Build	Some research & development Selective mass promotion Heavy personal selling
Food Processing	Nicher	Build or Hold	Selective mass promotion Other sales promotion Some personal selling Heavy price competition
Health Food Line	Nicher	Hold	Selective mass promotion Selective distribution Heavy price competition Some personal selling

*For a discussion of Leader, Challenger, Follower and Nicher strategies, see Kotler (1994).

Exhibit 12–6   Key Components of the Marketing Plan for Company X

Exhibit 12–6 illustrates the relationships among the goals, game plans, and marketing plans. This is only a brief outline. Its primary purpose is to illustrate what the marketing decision maker must confront. Therefore, it must not be construed as presenting simple solutions for complicated problems. In every stage of the decision-making process, an information base needs to be present so that decisions can be made swiftly and effectively. These will enable the firm to optimize its market opportunities. In the case of Company X, it is necessary to point out that in addition to "build" and "hold," the firm may have the options of harvest, retrench, and divest. These are not shown in Exhibit 12–6. It must be reiterated that throughout this book the basic intention is to illustrate and explain the key connections among data, information, and action. Most marketing management textbooks are likely to have more complete and, perhaps, exhaustive lists of actions, but in essence, they do not emphasize this three-stage relationship. As already seen in Exhibit 12–5, in each decision stage, an information base must provide the necessary support.

Details of the "4 Ps"

The "4 Ps"—product, place, price, and promotion—are the firm's key weapons to establish and maintain a competitive edge. Once the parameters of the marketing plan have been established (Exhibit 12–5), it is necessary to put together the details of this marketing plan in terms of the specifics of the "4 Ps." Exhibit 12–7 provides some of the highlights of the marketing mix (the combination of the "4 Ps" to implement the overall marketing plan and the firm's game plan), decisions and corresponding information needs. Once again, the marketing decision maker is the person who must be involved in the decision-making process and therefore must articulate the information needs. As mentioned throughout the book, the decision maker must understand what research can do so that the information needs can be specified clearly.

Since having products or services that the market desires is the reason and the justification for the firm's existence, the firm must be constantly involved in product research. This implies, not only generating new product ideas and developing them (Samli, Palda, & Barker 1987; Kotler 1994), but establishing the feasibility and prioritization of products. All products do not have equal value to the firm on the basis of something similar to Boston Consulting Group's (BCG) product portfolio analysis (Kotler 1994). All the products and services must be analyzed periodically. Making room for new products may require elimination of certain marginal products (or "dogs," in BCG terminology). Such analyses require elaborate inputs from the firm's information system. This system naturally takes the shape and the form that the company puts on these key decision areas. If the information system is designed so that very specific information regarding the firm's competitive edge, based on its product decisions, can be improved, then this aspect of the IS is very important and positive. Almost all the items specified under the product decisions related information needs are standard concepts available in basic textbooks. Needless to say, the marketing decision maker must work together with the research group to decide the most appropriate specifics of this information system.

The last item in this section needs some elaboration. In certain cases, a product's contribution to the profit picture cannot be assessed directly since there may be secondary impact on the profit picture. If, for instance, a product is used as a "loss leader" (a low-priced product that attracts a lot of customers), that product's contribution to the profit picture is not how much it contributes to the profit picture, but how effective it is in attracting customers. Similarly, many products interact jointly and influence the market on this basis. This is why research related to the effectiveness of product groups is so critical. There must be ways to measure the *synergistic* impact of each product to the product line and, of course, to the well-being of the firm.

The second decision area in Exhibit 12–7 is place. Marketing decision makers, all too often, become overly involved in promoting the product to increase the sales volume rather than distributing the product more efficiently and reducing distribution costs. Research activity provides critical information relating to transportation, warehousing, inventory control and location activity relating to the firm's products individually and as product lines.

Price research probably is the least used and least advanced of marketing research activities. There is much tendency to rely on cost-accounting inputs rather than marketing inputs. However, the market's response to different price levels is quite different. Therefore, it is necessary to approximate demand elasticities that will direct future price adjustments. If, for instance, demand is elastic, then it will not be wise to raise the price. Instead, it may be more realistic to enhance the promotion activity or perhaps even cut the price slightly. Similarly, price research is particularly important for new products. Again, being bound by costs is not too wise since the market's perception of value is quite different than the cost of production or the company's own perception of value. There are many research techniques, and there has been much research done in these areas. Continuing such research and utilizing its results for marketing decisions are very critical functions that are among the responsibilities of marketing decision makers.

In Exhibit 12–7, three important price research areas and corresponding information needs are specified. Certainly, pricing area related research can be substantially more involved, but these areas are among the most critical.

Finally, the promotional decision-related activity is extremely critical. In the market system those firms that are not capable of entering the vast communication networks of the markets cannot possibly survive (Samli & Bahn 1992). Some of the most difficult research questions in marketing are in this area. Little is known about the direct impact of promotional activity. In essence, demand elasticity needs to be compared with promotion elasticity, namely, would lowering the price be more or less effective in stimulating the demand than increasing promotional activity? Furthermore, it is equally difficult to determine the TV advertising equivalence of, say, radio advertising. In other words, what is the best promotional mix? Additionally, there are certain ranges within which the firm benefits substantially from promotional activity. It is extremely critical that the marketing decision-maker establish such ranges. Finally, a special reference is made in Exhibit 12–7 to task-objective budgeting. In establishing a promotional budget, all too often there is a tendency to establish a sum and break it down into different promotional functions. However, the promotional budget must reflect the specific activities of the firm to satisfy its needs to communicate in the marketplace. Therefore, not a breakdown but rather a buildup method of budgeting is needed (Samli 1989). Task-objective budgeting reflects such an approach. All necessary promotional activities are first

Product Decisions	Information Needs
Which products should be developed and supported	Product feasibility and product performance
Market power of existing product lines	Product image, brand image comparisons, growth and market saturation information
Declining products revitalization versus discarding	Product's contribution to the profit picture, market attitude toward products
Relationship among product lines	Product image, brand image comparisons, product's contribution to the profit picture.
Place Decisions	
Do our products have adequate market exposure	Product-retail outlet relationship; product image-store image congruence
Are our physical distribution costs in order	Physical distribution research relating to transportation, storage, inventory control and location decisions
Do our channels of distribution function well	Comparative channel information, cost-sales comparisons
Price Decisions	
Are price levels for our products reasonable	Product revenues and price elasticity analyses; cost versus revenue relationships; price perceived quality
Would changes in price improve the profit picture without strong reaction from competitors	Demand elasticity, price and revenue relationships for our products and for our competitors (if possible)
How important is the price in the minds of the customers? Is it related to their conception of value?	Price sensitivity of the customers, price perceived quality research, prices of product groups versus individual products in the group
Promotion Decisions	
What is the most reasonable promotion mix	The sales revenue dollars, impact of advertising personal selling, sales promotion and other public relations activity
What are the limits of promotional activity	Market potentials versus advertising outlays
What is an optimum promotional budget	The components of the promotional mix that will provide adequate market power; data for task-objective budgeting

Exhibit 12–7   Some Key Decision Areas and Corresponding Information Needs in the "4 Ps"

listed, and then a price tag is attached to each. The sum total of these price tags will indicate the total budget.

SUMMARY

Marketing research and information generation are solely designed to facilitate the marketing decision maker's particular needs. In this chapter, the firm's information system and its information needs were analyzed in conjunction with the series of marketing decision processes. First, a discussion was presented regarding the premarketing strategy decision sequence. Five specific steps were identified: opportunities, threats, strengths, weaknesses, and priorities. In the second part of the chapter, the marketing strategy and management plan were analyzed. Here four sequential stages were considered: goals, general game plan, marketing game plan, and marketing management plan, which means deciding on the details of the "4 Ps." The last section of the chapter dealt very specifically with the decision areas and information needs of the "4 Ps."

REFERENCES

Cravens, David W. 1994. *Strategic Marketing*. Burr Ridge, IL: Richard D. Irwin.

Granger, C. W. J. 1989. *Forecasting in Business and Economics*. San Diego, CA: Academic Press.

Jain, Subhash C. 1993. *Marketing Planning and Strategy*. Cincinnati: South-Western Publishing Co.

Kotler, Philip. 1994. *Marketing Management*. Englewood Cliffs, NJ: Prentice-Hall.

Kotler, Philip, Liam Fahey, and S. Jatusripitak. 1985. *The New Competition*. Englewood Cliffs, NJ: Prentice Hall.

Samli, A. Coskun. 1989. *Retail Marketing Strategies*. Westport, CT: Quorum Books.

———.1993. *Counterturbulence Marketing*. Westport, CT: Quorum Books.

Samli, A. Coskun, and Kenneth Bahn. 1992. "An Alternative Theory of the Market: A Meta Theoretical Approach." *Journal of the Academy of Marketing Science* 20 (Special Edition on Marketing Theory, Spring): 143–54.

Samli, A. Coskun, Kristian Palda, and Tansu Barker. 1987. "Toward a Mature Marketing Concept." *Sloan Management Review*, Winter, 45–51.

Using Information for Control Purposes

Marketing takes place in the market. It is important to determine the effectiveness of a firm's marketing activities so that they can be improved, changed, or maintained. This feedback function is essential to control the market performance of the firm. Of course, this can be performed through the use of financial information and marketing performance–related information.

Since all of a firm's activities are reflected in its profit picture, its financial performance should indicate the effectiveness of its marketing performance. However, it must be understood that the financial results are always obtained after the fact. Unless the firm can take early corrective action through proper market information, the financial results may indicate, for instance, that the firm has lost a lot of money. At this point, after the fact, this type of feedback occured too late. Traditional control systems based on feedback are not quite adequate since they take place after the event (Morgan 1992). On the other hand, early performance indicators can trigger the control mechanism for corrective action. This chapter presents a case for the use of marketing research for feedback-induced corrective action or control.

THE NEED TO DETERMINE EFFECTIVENESS

Samli (1993, 50) gave the following examples:

> The manager of X restaurant usually comes to work and finds a line of people waiting for his establishment to open. One morning, as he comes to work, he realizes that there's no longer a line waiting to go to X restaurant.

The customers of the retail establishment Y usually come in, browse around, and, typically, buy a number of things. Lately, of the people who come in and browse, only a very few buy something in the store.

The Z bank recently realized that many of its elderly customers (who happen to be a majority of its customers) have been leaving the bank without giving any reason.

These are just simple examples of early indicators of the firm's effectiveness. Their importance lies in the fact that they provide an early warning as to the firm's marketing performance. If any of these early indicators were to reflect the market realities for the firm, then measures for corrective action could be put in place quickly. If the firm did not have such early indicators to determine its market effectiveness, the same results would be seen in the financial statements of the firm at the end of the fiscal period. However, by the time the financial results are out, it would be too late to take corrective action. Thus, it is extremely critical for marketing decision makers, with the help of researchers, to develop unique early indicators. Samli and Barker (1984) pointed out that one of the most important strengths that can be attributed to marketing in a corporation is its ability to generate information that can be used as early indicators. Each firm has certain unique features and market relationships that will provide early indicators.

A MODEL OF MARKETING SYMPTOMATOLOGY

A model of marketing performance is presented in Exhibit 13–1. Much information is needed to develop the firm's marketing strategy. Chapter 12 dwelt on this topic. In preparing the strategic plan and implementing the strategy, the marketing decision maker must take into account a number of external uncontrollables, such as the competitor's actions, consumers' tastes, laws that are directing business transactions, among many others.

As the strategies are implemented by the use of marketing inputs such as the firm's image, its products, know-how, sales force, brands, patents, and the like, marketing impact emerges. This latter may take the form of the market's attitude toward the products, services, or distribution activities of the firm. The actual sales volume is another key marketing impact. The firm's market share, among many others, can also be used as indicators (Samli 1993).

As seen in Exhibit 13–1, the firm's marketing impact is determined by feedback composed of indicators and symptoms. A distinction is made here between indicators and symptoms. It must be said that all symptoms are indicators, but all indicators are not symptoms. In the

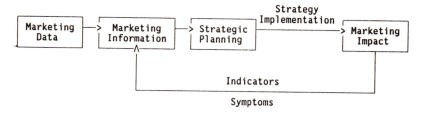

Source: Adopted and revised from Samli (1993).

Exhibit 13–1   A Model of Marketing Performance

case of the X restaurant above, not having a line waiting to get in is an indicator that does not relate directly to the problem. A symptom directly relates to a problem. For instance, if it were observed that customers entered the restaurant and looked at the menu and then walked out, obviously there is something wrong with the menu. Here, losing customers is the symptom related to the problem of the menu. This distinction between indicators and symptoms may be minor; however, it may also be important. The way it is discussed here implies that indicators may be detected even earlier than symptoms. Therefore, they are more general and may be related to multiple symptoms.

Detecting the negative impact through symptoms enhances the awareness of a total mechanism of chain reactions. Some years ago, the Audi 5000 automobile experienced some difficulties. When a number of customers reported that their Audis did not stop or went backward when they were supposed to go forward, the company did not pay attention to this symptom. Instead of pursuing this as an engineering problem, the president of Audi North America appeared on national television and accused those people of not knowing how to drive. The reaction of the market was negative. It put the progress of Audi in the U.S. market on hold. The company did not experience an increase in its sales volume of its market share. The early indication of user problems should have created a chain reaction of engineering corrections combined with an effective advertising campaign (Hulbert & Norman 1977; Samli 1993).

The necessary chain reaction as a result of the detected indicators and symptoms is illustrated in Exhibit 13–2. Monitoring the market performance of the firm is bound to yield early symptoms of the impact in the marketplace. Consider, for instance, a newly introduced auto model that in two months has amassed three times the repair bill of any newly

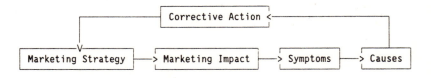

Exhibit 13–2 The Chain Reaction in Strategic Effectiveness. *Source:* Samli and Barker (1984).

introduced car in the past, in its particular category. If this symptom does not generate a chain reaction very quickly, the company stands to lose large sums of money. Similarly, a newly developed videocassette recorder may have four times the return rate that any videocassette recorder had in the past. The purchasers have been returning the equipment before the trial period is over and have registered their dissatisfaction. Once again, if this symptom is not quickly detected and corrective action not forthcoming, the firm will have a costly experience in the marketplace (Samli 1993). Sensing early symptoms can help determine the causes that would make it easier to activate the control mechanism through corrective action.

Federal Express has developed a *survey-feedback-action* program that includes internal climate surveys whereby subordinates review the management and workplace problem-solving initiatives. In order to administer such surveys, the company developed an electronic on-line survey system and implemented it for all of its employees. As a result, turnaround times are decreased and administrative errors are virtually eliminated (Smith 1993).

Modern computerized data gathering techniques such as Quick Response (QR) and Electronic Data Interchange (EDI) are used for *internal feedback* within the company to, again, improve the firm's general as well as specific performance. Feedback in such cases is used, for example, to improve the exchange of material and information between departments and companies. EDI and QR, along with bar codes, Optical Character Recognition (OCR), and other related technologies are helping the company to order material, schedule it, move it, and track it more effectively and efficiently. EDI, for instance, is providing the supplier with better, more timely feedback on what products are selling, where, and when. Additionally, it eliminates paperwork and the errors associated with manual data entries (Bushnell 1993).

PPG Industries, Inc., believes in quality extension by receiving unfiltered *feedback* from the customer. The company has established satellite supply facilities, applied the quality process to problem-solving, and provided multiple outlets for customer feedback. The company has developed a root-cause analysis that isolates and investigates materials, equipment, and human factors, and allows the company to quickly identify the real cause of the problem (Pullock 1993).

MARKETING SYMPTOMATOLOGY: A CLASSIFICATION

Symptoms indicating that a firm may be in serious trouble may be observed very closely. Similarly, symptoms pointing out that the firm is doing well must be identified and accounted for.

Marketing symptoms can be classified into three categories. The first is the marketing output—the actual performance record of management. By following this performance record, it is possible to detect certain symptoms of problems that are in the making. Americans did not like it when Coke Classic was taken out of the market and new Coke was introduced. Thanks to the company's information system, the situation was rectified quickly.

The second category is inputs. By analyzing the key marketing inputs, certain problems can be uncovered. Perhaps, even prior to output symptoms, the input symptoms may indicate potential problems. For instance, a pretest stage may indicate that a new product may be hazardous to health, or company A's product may not compare favorably with that of company B. Similarly, a panel or consumer focus group response may not be favorable to a company's newly proposed advertising campaign. Marketing decision makers must rely heavily on these and other early symptoms based on marketing inputs. By doing so they improve the opportunities of preventing or eliminating major problems that may be in the making (Samli 1993). These problems can be prevented very early by acting on these early indicators. Similarly, the firm can reallocate its resources more effectively by reinforcing very positive early indicators. Those areas that show great promise can be given more support to improve the firm's overall market performance.

The third category, unlike the first two sets of symptoms, is composed of more specific indicators dealing with inputs and outputs, occurring either one at a time or simultaneously. For instance, a firm may detect that its promotional messages are not congruent with each other; on the contrary, they are contradicting each other. This means the promotional messages that are meant to improve the firm's market position are not accomplishing their goals. They are simply offsetting each other. Hence, the firm is not making any progress and wasting large sums of money. Exhibit 13–3 illustrates some of these symptoms and the corresponding information needs for the marketing decision makers.

OUTPUT SYMPTOMS

Exhibit 13–3 points out five output symptoms that are distinguished in this chapter.

Market Position

Market position is a good indicator of a firm's marketing effectiveness. Any company can assess its market position in many different ways. Once again, it is critical not to rely on financial indicators that are after the fact. The marketing decision maker must be in a position to decide the type of indicator that may be used effectively. Furthermore, it must be understood that the firm not only can determine its market position, but also can improve it. The faster the symptoms are identified, the quicker the corrective action triggered by the control mechanism. There are many different methods of determining the firm's market position. Multidimensional scaling is one such approach. Such a technique will put the firm in its perceived position vis-à-vis its competitors. Knowing the firm's position regarding, say, the value and the quality it provides for its customers in comparison with its competitors, can be very significant in evaluating its marketing efforts and providing redirection (Samli 1993).

Sales Volume

Long before the financial statements of the company appear, detailed analysis of sales volume indicates if the overall performance is in the right direction. More specific analyses of sales volume in terms of sales territories, salesforce, and product group sales performance can more specifically indicate the strengths and weaknesses of the firm within given economic conditions. Chapter 4 presents some of the research techniques and data generation activity in this area. It must be realized that the strengths and weaknesses that are identified are only at that particular point in time. Thus, these strengths and weaknesses may change as the nature or the intensity of the factors influencing the market conditions change (Samli 1993).

Repeat Sales

If a company's sales are increasing but only a very small proportion of the total is repeat sales, obviously there is a critical problem. Either people are not repeating their purchases because they are disenchanted with the product, or the competitors have just introduced better products, or support services of the firm are unsatisfactory. These, among

Symptoms	Information Needs
General Marketing Symptoms (output)	
1. Market position	The relative market position of the firm in terms of sales and market share.
2. Sales volume	Absolute and relative changes in sales volume.
3. Repeat sales	Customer satisfaction and loyalty to products and company.
4. Product-market match	Changing market segments and continuing examination of market position of products.
5. Corporate image changes	Constant monitoring of the corporate image.
General Marketing Symptoms (input)	
1. Specific policies versus economic conditions	Understanding the market response to the firm under the changing economic conditions.

A. Decreasing activity in recession
    B. Increasing prices in inflation
    C. Doing both in stagflation	

2. Wrong marketing goals	Determining if the marketing goals are compatible with the market realities.
3. Wrong positioning	Reevaluating the firm's products in regards to their market positioning.
4. Downsizing	The impact of organizational changes on the firm's marketing competency.
Specific Symptoms (both input and output)	
1. Incongruent promotional messages	Market's immediate reaction to promotions.
2. Marginal revenue of promotion	The cost-revenue relationships in promotional activity.
3. Increase in customer complaints	The reaction of customers to the company and its products.
4. Abnormal proportions in brand switching	Customers' brand loyalty versus their preference of our competitors' products.
5. Increased unit pricing causing volume decline	Establishing optimal volume-price relationships.
6. Product mix changing in the wrong direction	Reassessment of the product mix in regards to changing market realities.

Source: Adapted and revised from Samli (1993).

Exhibit 13–3 Some Key Strategic Symptoms and Corresponding Information Needs

many other similar causes, indicate a problem. It is quite possible, for instance, that while the firm's products may be extremely appealing at the outset, they have some basic defect or design deficiency. The buyers, therefore, do not remain happy with them, and do not come back for repeat purchases (Samli 1993). The firm's information system must be extremely alert to identify such problems.

Product Market Match

It is of the utmost importance that the product (or products) match the market needs. These matches do not remain the same. As there are major changes in the firm's markets, chances are that there will be serious problems in its products satisfying the newly modified market needs. Product-market mismatches are extremely dangerous. Attitude surveys, observation studies, and other related research activity can easily identify these important changes in the firm's markets.

Corporate Image Changes

When, many years ago, DuPont managed to successfully switch its image from "producers of death" to "better things for better living through chemistry," the company gained more acceptance by the market and improved its overall market performance. Similarly, the image could be deteriorating and such a trend, unchecked, could eventually lead to the demise of the firm (Samli 1993). Once again, the firm's information system must uncover such developments to provide an opportunity for reinforcement or for remedial action.

INPUT SYMPTOMS

Four special input symptoms are identified in Exhibit 13–3. It must be reiterated that these are only a few examples. There can be many more similar or dissimilar symptoms that the marketing decision maker can use.

Specific Policies versus Economic Conditions

Input symptoms are clearly the beginning of more proactive marketing programs. As economic conditions change, performance of the firm changes as well. However, a corporate slowdown based on economic recession should be separated from an internal problem causing a decline in sales. A proactive behavior on the part of the marketing decision maker must be in a position to understand just what factors in the economy have direct influence of the firm's sales. So that the internal causes for a decline in the sales volume can be distinguished from the external causes that are creating the same results.

Wrong Marketing Goals

As market conditions change, the basic corporate goals may become inappropriate. Changing competitive conditions and the nature of the domestic economy caused A&P, the largest grocery chain in the United States, to experience significant annual losses. The chain had an unrealistic goal of being number one at any cost. A similar experience was registered by Sears Roebuck & Company. The company took its position of being the number one merchandiser of the world for granted and diversified into major financial areas. Thus, it lost its focus in retailing and consumer satisfaction. As a result, the company has been facing critical financial hardship (Samli 1993). There are many examples such as these. It is up to marketing decision makers to decide whether their marketing goals are realistic and compatible with the existing market realities. It is important that the firm's information system provide such critical information.

Wrong Positioning

The firm that positions itself in the marketplace erroneously is bound to lose. If, for instance, a pharmaceutical firm were to position itself as an outstanding researcher and a futuristic company and were to come up with a harmful new product that is based on poor research, that can be very damaging. The company can be irreparably damaged. A constant monitoring of the firm's products and its image can be a major prevention technique for such developments.

Downsizing

In recent years, the concept of downsizing has emerged as a fiscally responsible activity. However, downsizing and other organizational changes can be a critical problem if they do not carefully consider the firm's competency in the marketplace. Once again, the marketing decision maker must have enough research information to determine that the firm's marketing skills are intact despite any downsizing and reorganization efforts.

SPECIFIC SYMPTOMS

Exhibit 13–3 identifies six specific symptoms.

Incongruent Promotional Messages

The firm's promotional activity may either be unsuitable or may have become unsuitable for its target market. The bank that is trying to communicate with the upper middle class but succeeding in communicating only with the lower-middle class, for instance, is likely to become more and more ineffective as it continues to operate in the same manner. Furthermore, it may begin to lose money. In this case, the bank's information system must have a reading on the market's immediate reaction to its promotional activities.

Marginal Revenue of Promotion

If the firm cannot approximate whether its advertising or other promotional efforts are paying off, then it will be in a difficult situation. The cost revenue relationships must be carefully established by the firm's information system.

Increase in Customer Complaints

If the firm's customers are complaining more often than before about some specific aspects of the firm's business, there appears to be a serious problem in the making. Some of the firm's customers will complain very early. Their opinions can be used to identify the problem more succinctly and determine remedial measures. The firm's information system must be very sensitive to such types of developments. Wylde (1994) maintained that letters from customers can provide a great diversity and depth of information. Based on the researcher's ability and sensitivity to such data, letters from customers can reveal customers' attitudes, beliefs, behaviors, and actions. Some firms try to make it easier for their customers to reach them. In this process, many are setting up toll-free 800 numbers. Ragu Foods, Inc., for example, uses its 800 line as a marketing tool. Inputs from calls are put on a data base and circulated throughout the company (Trumfio 1993).

Abnormal Proportion in Brand Switching

There is always a certain amount of brand switching in the marketplace. However, if the research indicates that there is an excessive amount of brand switching and that the firm's customers are abandoning the firm's products, there is a critical problem. It is necessary to compare and contrast the firm's brands with those of the competitors.

Increased Unit Pricing

Many firms use unit costing as a basis for their pricing decisions. However, if the economy is slow or there is a decline in demand, then the unit cost may go up. The result is decreased sales volume due to increased price. Unless the firm's information system can establish certain optimalities between the unit cost and demand, the firm could lose much money (Samli 1993).

Product Mixes

Just as in the case of the U.S. auto industry in the 1980s, while the economic, social, and political conditions all pointed in the direction of small and efficient U.S. cars, the industry insisted on making the traditional large cars, with only a few exceptions. As a result, it lost a large portion of its market to small foreign imports. A firm must reassess its product mix constantly against the changing market realities. If the product mix moves in the opposite direction of the market, the firm is likely to face critical adversities.

SUMMARY

The firm must have a good corrective action triggered by its control mechanism. Thus, marketing symptomatology is very critical for ongoing success.

In this chapter a case was made for establishing a series of symptoms to indicate the quality of the firm's market performance. Three sets of symptoms were identified: (1) general marketing symptoms related to output, (2) general marketing symptoms related to input, and (3) specific symptoms related to both input and output.

The most important point in this chapter is that marketing research is much faster than financial evaluation. By the time the financial results of a firm are out, it may have lost much money, an outcome that could have been avoided by developing and using early market indicators.

REFERENCES

Bushnell, Rick. 1993. "Include Logistics in Your Thinking." *Modern Materials Handling*, March, 31–33.

Hulbert, J. M., and E. T. Norman. 1977. "A Strategic Framework for Marketing Control." *Journal of Marketing* (April): 12–20.

Morgan, Malcolm J. 1992. "Feedforward Control for Competitive Advantage: The Japanese Approach." *Journal of General Management* (Summer): 41–52.

Pullock, E. Kears. 1993. "A Vigorous Approach to Customer Services." *Journal of Business Strategy* (January-February): 16–20.

Samli, A. Coskun. 1993. *Counterturbulence Marketing*. Westport, CT: Quorum Books.

Samli, A. Coskun, and A. Tansu Barker. 1984. "Early Diagnosis of Marketing Problems." *Management Forum*, March, 22–26.

Smith, Bob. 1993. "FedEx's Key to Success." *Management Review*, July, 23–24.

Trumfio, Ginger. 1993. "Hear Like It Is." *Sales and Marketing Management*, October, 26.

Wylde, Margaret A. 1994. "How to Read an Open Letter." *American Demographics*, September, 48–52.

Postscript

This book deals with the very important topic of making marketing decisions based on information. It even goes a step further and attempts to connect information to knowledge. In doing so, it posits that a learning atmosphere must prevail in the organizational setting in such a way that changes in organizational and marketing behavior will take place as needed or as dictated by the marketplace. Thus, it is critical to explore just how the marketing decision maker and marketing research activity can work together to enhance the market performance of the firm and, furthermore, how the information can be transformed into knowledge. Finally, we must know how all these concepts relate to the firm's strategic posture. In other words, the decision process of the firm is almost totally dependent on a *strategic information system* that is functional, accessible, and *decision maker–friendly*.

In recent years there has been an excessive reliance on computers for research and decision making. This book makes the point that while the computer is a wonderful servant, it is a questionable master. In other words, whereas the marketing decision maker can use information generated by the computer from the data, it may be dangerous to rely exclusively on it. This is because the computer does not have human characteristics, and marketing is not strictly a science. Although scientific data analyses can give the decision maker a head start and excellent ammunition, it is up to the decision maker to make the best decision. This requires not only the relevant information but also the experience and the wisdom to make the best decision.

This book attempts to establish the relationship between the marketing decision maker and the firm's information system. It also provides guidance for the marketing decision maker as to how to generate and use the information for decision making. The marketing decision maker is not a researcher yet he or she must understand research, what it can do, and what its limitations are. Unlike many marketing research books, it is posited here that the decision maker is primarily in charge and must be in a position to articulate the information needs. Hence, he or she has the information responsibility in the firm. However, the technical details are the research department's responsibility.

For the well-being of the firm, it is extremely important that both the marketing decision maker and the research group exercise mutual respect and keep the best interest of the firm in mind. This book deals with facilitating marketing decisions with better information. As markets become more complex and turbulent, the marketing decision process becomes more complicated and more information driven. Much needs to be done to bring information and marketing decisions together. Therein lies the importance of this book

Exhibit PS–1 illustrates the general areas where future explorations should concentrate. According to the exhibit, almost all the major areas in information generation and utilization need to be developed further. This is not to say that these areas are altogether undeveloped, but rather,

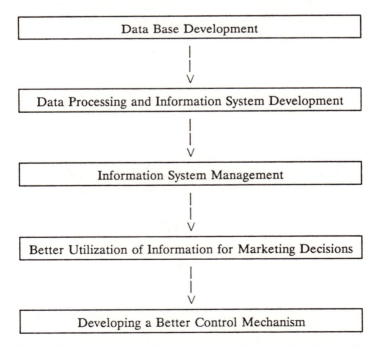

Exhibit PS–1 Future Areas of Exploration for Developing Better Corporate Information Systems

that gaining more sophistication will place a firm in an enhanced competitive position. The five areas that need to be developed further are (1) database development, (2) data-processing and information system development, (3) information system management, (4) better utilization of information in marketing decisions, and (5) a better control mechanism. Perhaps one additional component can be added to this list: the learning atmosphere. The information that is converted into knowledge should not leave the firm as its personnel leave. This is an additional challenge to both marketing and management (Slater & Narver 1994).

DATABASE DEVELOPMENT

The tremendous progress, during recent years, in the area of database development has been more in the direction of technology than user needs. Although database management activity thus far has been primarily technical, a more marketing-friendly version of this activity is in the making. However, much work remains to be done. Jackson and Wang (1994) maintained that new techniques will provide better understanding of the data behind the models and compare multiple techniques so that the marketing decision maker can pick the technique that is most appropriate. The database must be developed particularly in view of the information needs of the decision maker.

DATA PROCESSING AND INFORMATION SYSTEM DEVELOPMENT

Although the comments in the previous section are appropriate for this section as well, there is an additional, critical point to make. In developing an information system, the firm's decision-making needs must come first. Thus, the more qualified the decision makers, the more capable of identifying their information needs. Developing truly pertinent information from databases is one of the greatest challenges of both marketing researchers and marketing decision makers.

INFORMATION SYSTEM MANAGEMENT

As discussed in Chapter 10, managing the firm's information system is extremely important. The marketing decision maker must have immediate access to certain information, which must be up-to-date, in the needed format, and *interactive* in order to meet the specific needs of the decision maker.

BETTER UTILIZATION OF INFORMATION

If left alone, there is a tendency for decision makers and information personnel to go in different directions (Drucker 1989). This is, to say the least, an extremely dangerous development. Decision makers and information staff must constantly remain in close communication. Much needs to be done to determine how these two critical activities can be optimized. If one goes in its own direction and becomes increasingly distant from the other, the combination of the two is not likely to be optimized.

Much research is also needed regarding the improved use of information in marketing decisions. Much of the specifics of this point were presented in Exhibit 12–7. Information needs for many different marketing decisions may be identified, but the information may not be present. Similarly, the quality of the information may be in question. Thus, the goal is better utilization of *better* information. However, a key point needs to be reiterated: this book is about developing information systems for strategic marketing decisions. Therefore, it focuses on developing strategic marketing-information systems. Exhibit 12–7 does not distinguish between marketing management decision–related information and marketing strategy–related information. Much effort is needed in this area. It is quite possible that the future information systems for marketing may be divided into *marketing management information systems* and *strategic marketing information systems*. The two may be distinguished in terms of organization, data generation, management, and delivery procedures.

DEVELOPING A BETTER CONTROL MECHANISM

Unfortunately, even though they are deficient (Chapter 13), financial indicators are more popular than marketing indicators. Thus, it is extremely important to develop techniques to construct good marketing indicators. Marketing symptomatology is a very inadequately developed area. Clearly, we need a theory and research methodology to trigger corrective action. It is certainly hoped that this book will stimulate the imagination and professionalism of both marketing researchers and marketing decision makers. They must work together to benefit themselves, their companies, and the society as a whole.

REFERENCES

Drucker, Peter. 1989. *The New Realities*. New York: Harper and Row.

Jackson, Rob, and Paul Wang. 1994. *Strategic Database Marketing*. Lincolnwood, IL: NTC Business Books.

Slater, Stanley F., and John C. Narver. 1994. *Market Oriented Isn't Enough: Build a Learning Organization*. Report no. 94–103. Cambridge, MA: Marketing Science Institute.

Selected Bibliography

Aaker, David A., and George S. Day. 1990. *Marketing Research*. New York: John Wiley and Sons.

Alderson, Pat. 1993. "Managing the Costs of On-Line Information." *Best's Review*, July, 74–78.

Alter, Steven L. 1980. *Decision Support Systems*. Reading, MA: Addison-Wesley.

Bagozzi, Richard P. 1980. *Causal Models in Marketing*. New York: John Wiley and Sons.

Barthes, R. 1967. *Elements of Semiology*. London: Cape.

Bigant, J., and Y. Rickebusch. 1985. "Marketing Research in France." *European Research* 13(1) (January): 4–11.

Blount, Steve. 1992. "Test Marketing: It's Just a Matter of Time." *Sales and Marketing Management*, March, 32–43.

Brennan, Leslie. 1988. "Special Supplement—Test Marketing." *Sales and Marketing Management*, March, 50–62.

Bushnell, Rick. 1993. "Include Logistics in Your Thinking." *Modern Materials Handling*, March, 31–33.

Collins, Leslie F. 1991. "Everything Is True, But in a Different Sense: A New Perspective on Qualitative Research." *Journal of the Market Research Society* (January): 31–38.

Cooley, W. W., and P., R. Lohnes. 1971. *Multivariate Data Analysis*. New York: John Wiley and Sons.

Cooper, P. and A. Branthwaite. 1977. "Qualitative Technology: New Perspectives on Measurement and Meaning through Qualitative Research." In *Proceedings*, 79–92. Brighton, U.K.: MRS Conference.

Cravens, David W. 1982. *Strategic Marketing*. Homewood, IL: Richard D. Irwin.

Davies, Richard. 1986. "Omnibus Surveys." In *Consumer Market Research Handbook*, ed. Robert T. Worchester and John Downham, 231–44. Amsterdam: ESOMAR, North Holland.

de Souza, M. 1984. "For a Better Understanding of Individuals: Non-Verbal Approaches." In *Proceedings*, 163–76. Copenhagen, Denmark: EMAC/ESOMAR Symposium on Methodological Advances in Marketing Research Theory and Practice.

Drucker, Peter. 1989. *The New Realities*. New York: Harper and Row.

Fane, Gary. 1992. "Into the Future: The Controller as Marketer." *Corporate Controller*, January/February, 25–30.

Fleury, P. 1984. "New Qualitative Studies." In *Proceedings*, 629–47. Rome, Italy: ESOMAR Congress, September.

Ford, Gary T. 1974. "A Multivariate Investigation of Market Research." In *1974 Combined Proceedings*, ed. Ronald C. Curhan, 177–81. Chicago: American Marketing Association.

Frontori, L., A. Pogliana, and B. Spataro. 1984. "Application of Play-Oneiric Tests in Basic Motivational Research and Communication Studies." In *Proceedings*, 649–68. Rome, Italy: ESOMAR Congress, September.

Fuld, Leonard M. 1992. "Achieving Total Quality through Intelligence." *Long Range Planning*, February, 109–15.

Glaser, Rashi, and Allen M. Weiss. 1993. "Marketing in Turbulent Environments: Decision Processes and the Time-Sensitivity of Information." *Journal of Marketing Research* (November): 509–21.

"The Gold Mine of Data in Customer Services." 1994. *Business Week*, March 21, 113–14.

Goyder, John. 1966. "Surveys on Surveys: Limitations and Potentialities." *Public Opinion Quarterly* 50:27–41.

Granger, C. W. J. 1989. *Forecasting in Business and Economics*. San Diego, CA: Academic Press.

Green, P. E., M. H. Halbert, and P. J. Robinson. 1966. "Canonical Analysis: An Exposition and Illustrative Application." *Journal of Marketing Research* (February).

Green, Paul E., R. E. Frank, and P. J. Robinson. 1967. "Cluster Analysis in Test Market Selection." *Management Science* (April): 387–400.

Gronroos, Christian. 1990. *Service Management and Marketing*. Lexington, MA: Lexington Books.

Grove, Stephen J., and Raymond P. Fisk. 1992. "Observational Data Collection Method for Services Marketing: An Overview." *Journal of the Academy of Marketing Science* (Summer): 217–24.

Haeckel, Stephen H., and Richard L. Nolan. 1993. "Managing by Wire." *Harvard Business Review* (September-October): 122–32.

Haire, M. 1950. "Projective Techniques in Marketing Research." *Journal of Marketing* 14 (April): 649–56.

Hawkins, Del I., Roger J. Best, and Kenneth A. Coney. 1989. *Consumer Behavior—Implications for Marketing Strategy*. Homewood, IL: BPI-Irwin.

Jackson, Rob, and Paul Wang. 1994. *Strategic Database Marketing*. Lincolnwood, IL: NTC Business Books.

Jain, Subhash C. 1993. *Marketing Planning and Strategy*. Cincinnati: South-Western Publishing Co.

Kavan, C. Bruce, Cheryl J. Frohlich, and A. Coskun Samli. 1994. "Developing a Balanced Information System." *Journal of Services Marketing* 8(1): 4–13.

Kendall, M. G. 1975. *Multivariate Analysis*. New York: Hafner Press.

Kotler, Philip. 1994. *Marketing Management*. Englewood Cliffs, NJ: Prentice-Hall.

Kotler, Philip, Liam Fahey, and S. Jatusripitak. 1985. *The New Competition*. Englewood Cliffs, NJ: Prentice-Hall.

Krum, James R., Pradeep A. Rau, and Stephen K. Keiser. 1987–1988. "The Marketing Research Process." *Journal of Advertising Research* (December/January): 9–21.

Lilien, Gary L., Philip Kotler, and K. Sridhar Moorthej. 1992. *Marketing Models*. Englewood Cliffs, NJ: Prentice-Hall.

Luck, David J. 1974. *Marketing Research*. Englewood Cliffs, NJ: Prentice-Hall.

Mentzer, John T., and Nimish Gandhi. 1992. "Expert Systems in Marketing: Guidelines for Development." *Journal of the Academy of Marketing Science* (Winter): 73–80.

Montgomery, David B., and Charles B. Weinberg. 1979. "Toward Strategic Intelligence Systems." *Journal of Marketing* 41–52.

Morgan, Malcolm J. 1992. "Feedforward Control for Competitive Advantage: The Japanese Approach." *Journal of General Management* (Summer): 41–52.

Myers, James H., and A. Coskun Samli. 1969. "Management Control of Marketing Research." *Journal of Marketing Research* (August): 267–77.

Naisbitt, John. 1982. *Megatrends*. New York: Warner Books.

Packard, V. O. 1957. *The Hidden Persuaders*. New York: David McKay.

Peters, Tom. 1989. *Thriving on Chaos*. New York: Alfred A. Knopf.

Pullock, E. Kears. 1993. "A Vigorous Approach to Customer Services." *Journal of Business Strategy* (January-February): 16–20.

Samli, A. Coskun. 1967. "Observations as a Means of Fact Gathering for Marketing Decisions." *Business Perspectives*, Fall, 19–24.

———. 1985. "International Strategic Information Systems." In *Proceedings*. Miami, FL: Second World Marketing Congress, Academy of Marketing Science.

———. 1989. *Retail Marketing Strategies*. Westport, CT: Quorum Books.

———. 1992. *Social Responsibility in Marketing*. Westport, CT: Quorum Books.

———. 1993. *Counterturbulence Marketing*. Westport, CT: Quorum Books.

Samli, A. Coskun, and Kenneth Bahn. 1992. "An Alternative Theory of the Market: A Meta Theoretical Approach." *Journal of the Academy of Marketing Science* 20 (Special Edition on Marketing Theory, Spring): 143–54.

Samli, A. Coskun and A. Tansu Barker. 1984. "Early Diagnosis of Marketing Problems." *Management Forum*, March, 22–26.

Samli, A. Coskun, and Cheryl Frohlich. 1992. "Service: The Competitive Edge in Banking." *Journal of Services Marketing* (Winter): 15–22.

Samli, A. Coskun, Kristian Palda, and Tansu Barker. 1987. "Toward a Mature Marketing Concept." *Sloan Management Review*, Winter, 45–51.

Samli, A. Coskun, Enid Tozier, and Yvett Harps. 1978. "Social Class Differences in the Apparel Purchase Behavior of Single, Professional Black Women." *Journal of the Academy of Marketing Science* (Spring): 25–38.

Sampson, P. 1985. "Qualitative Research in Europe: The State of the Art and Art of the State." In *Broadening the Uses of Research*, Proceedings of the 38th ESOMAR Congress, 67–99. Wiesbaden, Germany.

Schaderbek, Charles G. 1985. *Management Systems: Conceptual Considerations*. Plano, TX: Business Publications.

Schiffman, L. G., and L. L. Kanuk. 1983. *Consumer Behavior*. 2nd ed. Englewood Cliffs, NJ: Prentice-Hall.

Seeling, Pat. 1989. "All over the Map." *Sales and Marketing Management*, March, 58–64.

Sheth, J. N. 1969. "Application of Multivariate Methods in Marketing." In *Marketing and the New Science of Planning*, ed. R. L. King, 259–65. Chicago: American Marketing Association.

Sinkula, James M. 1994. "Market Information Processing and Organizational Learning." *Journal of Marketing* (January): 35–45.

Slater, Stanley F., and John C. Narver. 1994. *Market Oriented Isn't Enough: Build a Learning Organization*. Report no. 94–103. Cambridge, MA: Marketing Science Institute.

Stafford, Marla Royne. 1993. "Participant Observation and the Pursuit of Truth: Methodological and Ethical Considerations." *Journal of the Marketing Research Society* (January): 63–76.

Stern, Aimee L. 1991. "Testing Goes Industrial." *Sales and Marketing Management*, March, 30–40.

Stevens, S. S. 1946. "On the Theory of Scales of Measurement." *Science*, June 7, 677–80.

Watters, Carolyn, and Michael A. Shepherd. 1994. "Shifting the Information Paradigm from Data-Centered to User-Centered." *Information Processing and Management* 30(4): 455–71.

Wedberg, George H. 1990. "But First, Understand the Problem." *Journal of Systems Management* (June): 20–28.

Weiers, Ronald M. 1984. *Marketing Research: A Structure for Decisions*. Reading, MA: Addison-Wesley.

Index

ABOUT THE AUTHOR

Dr. A. Coskun (Josh) Samli is Research Professor of Marketing and International Business at the University of North Florida. He received his bachelor's degree from Istanbul Academy of Commercial Science; his M.B.A. is from the University of Detroit and his Ph.D. is from Michigan State University. As a Ford Foundation fellow, he did post-doctoral work at the University of Chicago and as an International Business Program fellow at New York University.

In 1974–1975, he was Sears-AACSB Federal Faculty Fellow in the Office of Policy and Plans, U.S. Maritime Administration. In 1983, Dr. Samli was invited to New Zealand as the Erskine Distinguished Visiting Scholar to lecture and undertake research at Canterbury University. In 1985, Dr. Samli was a Fulbright Distinguished Lecturer in Turkey. He was selected as the Beta Gamma Sigma, L. J. Buchan Distinguished Professor for the academic year 1986–1987.

Dr. Samli is the author or coauthor of more than two hundred scholarly articles, eight books, and thirty monographs. He has been invited, as a distinguished scholar, to deliver papers in more than a dozen universities and has lectured extensively in Europe, Eastern Europe, the Middle East, the Far East, Oceania, South Africa, and many other parts of the world. He has been very active in the Fulbright Commission and is on the review board of seven major journals.

Dr. Samli is a Senior Fellow in the Academy of Marketing Science. He conducted some of the earlier studies on the poor, the elderly, and price discrimination. His most recent books published by Quorum are *Social Responsibility in Marketing* (1992), *Counterturbulence Marketing* (1993), and *International Consumer Behavior* (1995).

ISBN 0-89930-976-3